SANSKRIT STUDIES

Owing to the antiquity and rarity of this book, certain pages are regrettably absent, and readability is compromised due to the blurring of the original text. If you possess any insights regarding the availability of these missing sections, kindly inform us. Your assistance is crucial in ensuring the completion of this significant work for the benefit of future generations.

SANSKRIT STUDIES

M. HIRIYANNA

GYAN

Published by

GYAN

Gyan Publishing House
5, Ansari Road
Daryaganj, New Delhi-110002
Phone: 011-47034999, 9811692060
E-mail: books@gyanbooks.com

Distribution Network
gyanbooks.com
India, USA, Canada, UK, Australia

ISBN: 978-93-6920-232-4 (PB)

First Published, 1954

2nd Impression 2025

Printed at: Gyan Press, Delhi.

SANSKRIT STUDIES
Author: M. HIRIYANNA

By M. Hiriyanna

POPULAR ESSAYS IN INDIAN PHILOSOPHY

THE QUEST AFTER PERFECTION

ART EXPERIENCE

SANSKRIT STUDIES

BY

M. HIRIYANNA

KAVYALAYA PUBLISHERS
MYSORE

PUBLISHERS' NOTE

Some papers of a general nature relating to Sanskrit literature and language, of the late Prof. Hiriyanna have been brought together in this volume. Except the first and the last essay, the rest have appeared in various journals and publications. The last, *The Study of Sanskrit*, is an address delivered on the occasion of the inauguration of the Sanskrit Association of the Maharaja's College, Mysore, during the year 1916. *Sanskrit Poetry: A Historical Retrospect* appears to be one of the early papers of the author. The editors found it necessary to omit a few sentences from the text of this paper and these omissions are indicated by dots in the text. Keith's *Classical Sanskrit Literature* was reviewed by the author for two journals, *The Mysore University Magazine* and the *Journal of the Karnataka Sahitya Parishat.* Hence ideas appearing in the former review have been omitted from the latter to avoid repetition. These omissions are also indicated by dots. Words or sentences added by the editors either in the body of the text or in the footnotes are enclosed within square brackets.

We are grateful to Prof. Hiriyanna's daughter for having permitted us to publish these studies. Our grateful thanks are also due to Prof. T. N. Sreekantaiya of the Karnatak University, Dharwar and Sri N. Sivarama Sastry of the University of Mysore who have rendered us all possible help in the editing of these *Studies*.

ACKNOWLEDGMENTS

The late Prof. Hiriyanna's daughter desires to express her grateful thanks to the Editors of the *Indian Review* and the *Journal of the Karnataka Sahitya Parishat* and the Registrar of the *University of Mysore*, for their courtesy in allowing her to include in the present collection the several articles first published by them.

M.R.

FIRST PUBLICATION

'Vision of Vāsavadattā'—*Indian Review, October 1929.*

Kālidāsa—*The Maharaja's College Magazine, September 1913.*

The Vocabulary of the 'Meghasandeśa'—Foreword to *Padāvali of the Meghasandeśa* and *Kuntaleśvara-dautya of Kālidāsa.* Compiled by His Holiness Sri Yatiraja Sampatkumara-Ramanujamuni of Melkote (Mysore). Published by A. Srinivasa Iyengar, Sri Yatiraja Mutt, Melkote 1939.

'Mālatī and Mādhava'—*Indian Review, August 1930.*

'Uttara-Rāmacarita' — *The Mysore University Magazine, February 1917.*

'Classical Sanskrit Literature'—*The Mysore University Magazine, September 1924. Journal of the Karnataka Sahitya Parishat, July 1924.*

'A History of Sanskrit Literature'—*The Mysore University Magazine, March 1929.*

CONTENTS

SANSKRIT STUDIES

SANSKRIT POETRY: A HISTORICAL RETROSPECT

To the well-known difficulty of treatment which is inherent in all art, there is to be added in the case of Sanskrit Poetry, another arising from the immensity of its range. Poems in Sanskrit are to be counted by hundreds and they cover a period of several centuries especially if we include the Veda also within our purview. I need hardly point out that my purpose is not to survey the whole of this vast and difficult field. The task I have set myself this evening is much humbler. I wish to place before you two well-marked tendencies in Sanskrit poetry which bear to each other a relationship of historical sequence and to show that the change of ideal implied by them is in perfect harmony with the general development of mental life in ancient India. As a preliminary to what I shall say, I may remark that in matters like poetry which are the products of human feeling and thought, advance from one stage to another is never absolute and final. Owing to the ineradicable diversity of human temperament, whatever ideal once becomes deeply rooted in the social consciousness tends to persist ever afterwards and hence we find that the old is often preserved by the side of the new. Nevertheless each stage of development has its own dominant tendency through which we get an insight into the essential spirit of that stage.

The earliest Indian Poetry that has come down to us is found in the *Ṛgveda*. It is well known that this work consists of sacred songs and that its interest to a modern student is historical, not poetical. But at the same time, it would be incorrect to think that the work is devoid of aesthetic merit. Religious fervour everywhere gives rise to true poetry and India is not an exception to the rule. The *Ṛgveda* has a poetic side also and the poetical quality exhibited in some of the hymns is indeed very high. Vedic poetry, like Vedic religion with which it is closely connected, is the outcome of the personification of the visible powers of nature. The poets, no doubt, address these powers as gods but, generally speaking, there is no difficulty in discovering what natural objects and phenomena these gods represent. As one Western scholar has put it many of the Vedic gods are transparent. Thus the earliest poetry of India is at bottom nature-poetry in its simplest and purest form. The conditions of this paper do not permit of large extracts from the Veda being read, but yet to indicate some of the salient features of its poetry, I shall give in English a brief account of the Vedic description of Uṣas, the goddesss of Dawn, in portraying whose glory the ancient bards have exhibited their best poetic skill.

The Dawn is generally represented as the daughter of Heaven. Born in the eastern quarter of the firmament she places herself on the lap of Father Heaven and Mother Earth and fills them both with radiance. Night and day are her sisters. She is the bride of the far-darting sun. Clothed in pure and brilliant vesture she shines radiant by his side like a youthful wife in the presence of her husband. In another mood, the poets liken her, as she marches onward dispelling darkness, to a warrior casting his arrows or to a swift charger scattering enemies; and the rays that she sends to the extremities of the sky are figured as people arrayed in martial order, before whom the solid and odious glooms descend and disappear, seeking their abode. We have more direct pictures also of the Dawn. In shining light, before the wind arises, she comes gleaming over the waters and sets open the two gates of heaven. One poet says she illumes the world like congregated lightnings; another that she gives back all the regions. She softens the earth with balmy dews. She is the restorer of consciousness; the repository of sweetness. There are other passages which add a pathetic note to what is otherwise purely naturalistic poetry. For example one poet states that the divine and ancient Uṣas, born again and again and bright with unchanging hues, wastes away the life of mortals. Another poet crossing the border line between poetry and philosophy, which is always faint, cries out 'For how long a period is it that the Dawns have arisen? For how long a period will they rise? Those mortals who beheld the pristine Uṣas dawning have passed away; to us she is now visible; and they approach who may behold her in after times. She is exempt from decay or death and goes on for ever in her divine splendour'.

This poetry is such as may be expected to arise in a society which was in intimate communion with nature. There is nothing artificial here. Every thought springs naturally from the life which the poets led or beheld around them. So rich is this poetry in metaphor and allegory that it requires little effort on my part to show wherein its excellence lies. Nature is here presented to us suffused in a continual light of the poet's fancy whose power we feel not only in the bold personifications but also in the refreshing pictures of the physical aspects of the Dawn. Such imaginative renderings of nature cannot fail to give us that peculiar joy for which we almost instinctively go to works of art. We shall presently see what this joy signifies. But the point on which I like to lay special stress now is that this poetry has for its theme the beauty of nature and, *although its appeal to emotion is undoubted*, it does not make emotion its subject-matter.

By the side of these sacred hymns there must very early have sprung up secular poetry in the shape of epic tales and battle songs. There is allusion in ancient Sanskrit literature to the practice of professional minstrels entertaining ever-ready listeners in courts and hermitages by reciting such poetry to the accompaniment of music. It is poetry of this kind that should have furnished the chief material to the later epic writers and the *Mahābhārata* in particular should have been built up largely out of such songs. We have a few fragments of this secular poetry, preserved in the *Ṛgveda* itself, dealing with subjects like social customs, the liberality of patrons and so forth. These fragments also exhibit a mythological colouring implying thereby that the work of the lay artist at first resembled that of his brother, the religious bard, and either described the beauty of nature or recounted the outward activities of man. But in course of time a far-reaching change was introduced which gradually altered the very complexion of Indian poetry. We get a clue to the character of this change in the well-known story which is related at the beginning of the *Rāmāyaṇa* regarding the birth of Indian classical poesy. The circumstances associated with this event are attractive enough to bear reiteration. Vālmīki, a great sage of Kosala, was thinking of describing in a worthy manner the fortunes of Rāma, the divine hero of his country. Revolving this idea in his mind, he, one day went as usual to the river *Tamasā* to perform his mid-day ablutions. But on that day it so happened that he saw in the vicinity of the river a fowler killing one of a pair of lovely birds that were disporting themselves on the branch of a tree. The fowler singled out the male bird and brought it down with his arrow. Seeing the bird lie on the ground, weltering in its blood, its mate began to wail in plaintive tones. The soft-hearted sage was moved to intense pity at this sight; and his grief spontaneously burst forth in the form of a *śloka* which according to tradition, was the first rhythmic utterance outside the old archaic language of the Vedas.[1] Vālmīki looked upon this *śloka* as suggesting to him the key-note of his contemplated work and under the spell of its inspiration composed his great poem—the *Rāmāyaṇa*, and became celebrated as the *ādikavi*. Divested of its romantic elements this story signifies that a new poetic era dawned after the prosaic age of the Brāhmaṇas which had succeeded to the creative period of the *Ṛgveda* and that Vālmīki was the morning-star of Indian classical song.

The appearance of the *Rāmāyaṇa* marks a turning point in the history of the Indian language as well as in the history of Indian literature. It tells us in the first instance that what came to be known later as *Saṁskṛta* was for the first time raised to the dignity of a literary language by the efforts of Vālmīki. The old literary dialect of the Vedas had long fallen into disuse and poetic works had ceased to appear in it. Songs and ballads must indeed have been produced in the popular dialects of the day; but they could hardly take rank as literature. The popular dialects themselves had largely increased in number owing to the vastness of the territory occupied by the Aryans and the lack of a common medium of communication had also been strongly felt. But no *lingua franca* had as yet made its appearance. There was indeed one among the dialects distinguished for the transparency of its vocabulary, its regularity, flexibility and beauty of sound. But it could gain general currency only through its use by a poet of surpassing artistic genius. Vālmīki was such a poet; and by adopting that dialect as the medium of poetic expression he rendered to it the same service which Dante did to Italian or Chaucer to English. It thenceforward became the standard literary language, which character it has retained to this day, uniting in bonds of kinship communities which have spread themselves over the whole continent of India. The language which Vālmīki thus immortalised has ever since continued, substantially the same, and literature of

[1] [See, however, for a detailed discussion of the story, *Art Experience*, pp. 34 f.—Ed.]

the most varied character has never ceased to be produced in it.

The second point which the above story signifies is of far more importance to my present purpose. The occasion which gave birth to the *śloka* to which I have alluded was one of intense pathos and by placing it at the head of his *Rāmāyaṇa* Vālmīki indicates to us what he considered to be the central theme of his poem. For the first time, so far as our knowledge goes, emotion was deliberately adopted as the subject-matter of poetry; and as Vālmīki became the pattern for all future time in poetic matters Sanskrit writers turned their attention more and more from describing nature or the outward activities of man to the rendering of inward feeling. If we bear in mind that all classifications of literature can at best be only rough, we may say that Sanskrit poetry after Vālmīki became less descriptive and more lyrical. In other words, Emotion replaced Beauty as the theme of poetry. But what, it may be asked, is the meaning of making emotion the theme of poetry? Do not emotions, in their intrinsic character, belong to the order of the 'deep unspeakable'? It is true that they cannot be directly expressed. Words like 'fear' or 'anger' may name them but cannot describe them. Although emotions defy direct expression, they can be suggested by portraying those external features which are linked with them in our experience. That is all that the poet, who adopts emotions as his theme, does. By describing the outward and visible signs of particular states of feeling he rouses in us the experience of the corresponding stage. Thus the distinction between the old and new types of poetry is not merely one of content but also one of process; and it is the necessity for this indirect suggestion in the case of the later poetry that gave rise to the canon of *dhvani*, so celebrated in the history of Sanskrit criticism.

The distinction between the two types of poetry requires further elucidation. As regards their final effect there can of course be no difference, for both alike, as forms of art, must evoke aesthetic pleasure. But while the one achieves this result by describing external facts, the other does it by depicting internal feeling. This change does not mean a mere transfer of the poet's attention from nature to man, for the older poet did not stop at the description of nature but portrayed also the thoughts and activities of man. What distinguishes the later poet is that he delves deeper and utilises both nature and what I may call the 'outer man' as aids in revealing to us the inmost working of the human heart. The material to be poetised remains the same as before but it ceases to be the object of the poet's first regard. I shall illustrate my point by considering the place of nature in the later poetry. Since emotion is its exclusive theme, nature becomes a mere setting for it, instead of itself occupying the focus of the picture as it did in the Veda. The Indian poet does not indeed grow less sensible to the beauty of nature, nor does nature, in practice, figure less in the later poetry. But it ceases to be described for its own sake and becomes the means of attuning our mind to the emotion depicted. The details of nature chosen for portraying are determined, not by the requirements of an objective representation but by the character of the emotion to be subserved. The splendid and lavish descriptions of nature in the *Meghadūta* of Kālidāsa, for example, fully bear out this statement. Or take again the description of Kaṇva's hermitage in the first act of the same author's *Śākuntala*. As a picture of nature it can stand comparison with any of its kind. But the chief object of the poet in this description is not to afford us an external picture of the hermitage but to give us an insight into the inner feeling of serenity which reigns in the hearts of Kaṇva and his hermit disciples. So profound is this serenity that wild nature itself seems to have grown tame under its influence. If, as occasionally is the case, nature is pictured for its own sake, it is reckoned as *svabhāvokti*, an *alaṁkāra*—a mere embellishment which may, if required, be dispensed with. Thus what would be great poetry according to standards once prevalent is now relegated to quite a secondary place. What I have said of nature applies equally well to human thought and action in the later poetry. Like nature, they also constitute the outer vesture of poetry while the substance they clothe is Feeling. In fact Hindu critics group together everything other than emotion under the single head of *Vibhāvas* [and *anubhāvas*] or adjuncts to emotion. Beauty of nature, and beauty of human thought and action are found in both types of poetry but while the earlier points *to these* as its aim, the later points *from them* to something which lies deeper yet, viz., Feeling. Since Feeling may be regarded as the very fabric of our souls, we may designate the latter as 'Soul-poetry' in order to contrast it with the 'Nature-poetry' of the earlier stage.

This shifting of the poet's attention from the external to the internal world has its exact parallel in the history of Indian Philosophy and Religion. Indian philosophic thought began with the conception of Brahman as the first principle so far as it is comprehended in the outer universe and reached its culmination in identifying Brahman with *Ātman*, the first principle so far as it is known in the inner self of man. Similarly in Religion the old word for the god-head—'*deva*', which means 'shining', indicates that the early conception of divine power was derived from the luminous manifestations of outward nature while the later term *Īśā* or *Īśvara* signifies the *antaryāmin* who guides us from inside. This withdrawal from the outer reality to the internal is well illustrated by the following episode of Bālāki and Ajātaśatru which is preserved in the Upaniṣads. Bālāki was a learned but proud man. He once approached Ajātaśatru, king of Benares, and offered to teach him Brahman. Ajātaśatru was well pleased to have him at his court, for all the wise men were then going to Janaka, king of Mithilā, and settling at his court. He accordingly said to Bālāki, offering a gift as an inducement to stay—'We give you a hundred cows for that speech of yours, for verily all people run away saying Janaka is our patron'. Bālāki in course of time began to instruct the king and endeavoured several times in succession to define Brahman as the essence of the sun, the moon, lightning, wind, fire and so on, but in each case the king confuted his definition and said, 'This does not suffice to know the true Brahman'. Bālāki was silenced at last and the king, himself proceeding to instruct, took Bālāki by the hand and rose. The two together came to a person who was in deep sleep. The king called him by his name but he did not rise. Then he pushed him by the hand and woke him, pointing out to Bālāki at the same time, 'That in which the vital breaths were dormant in sleep is the Brahman'. The moral of this episode is the same as that implied by the change in the poet's attitude, viz., that as the Indian view of life deepened in course of time, the earlier naturalism yielded place to idealism.

To resume my subject after this digression. The new poetry is seen in its best form in the works of Kālidāsa and Bhavabhūti. But the *Meghadūta* of the former to which I have already referred represents to us the very acme of it. Here the poet describes the frustrated love between a Yakṣa and his consort and his thoughts are so much engrossed with that feeling that he ignores almost everything else. The plot all but reaches the vanishing point, there is only the faintest allusion to the incidents that lead up to the bitter disappointment; and the poet does not tarry even to mention the names of the hero and the heroine. Thus the poem has not a single prop to support it; and yet, its one hundred and odd stanzas have been, during fifteen centuries, regarded by all, not excluding the modern Sanskritist, as 'a perpetual feast of nectared sweets'.

A striking change like this in the poet's attitude could not have taken place on a sudden even when so mighty a genius as Vālmīki initiated it. . . . By the time of Kālidāsa, the new tendency had been firmly established and the predominance of emotion or 'unity of *rasa*' had come to be insisted upon as indispensable to poetic excellence. And it is not improbable that the example of Kālidāsa ensured its future. From Vālmīki's time to about Kālidāsa's, Sanskrit poetry may be taken to have been in a transition stage in which the place of emotion had not been finally settled. This circumstance affords us a fresh type of evidence for determining the age of a Sanskrit poem. Nothing of course that is based on so elusive a test as the aesthetic one can lead to any certainty of conclusion. Yet, other considerations apart, the lack of what I have termed 'unity of *rasa*' may be looked upon as presumptive evidence for the antiquity of a work. . . .

Although these two kinds of poetry are so different in scope, they both, according to the Indian conception of art, have the same end in view. To discover what this end is let us consider how we ordinarily view the world around and within us. Generally we look upon men and things in their relation to our purposes and grasp only such of their features as have a proximate or at least a remote bearing on our interests. We ignore all other features as having no meaning for us. If our conception of the external world is thus interested it is intensely more so in the case of our thoughts, feelings and actions. This self-interest gives rise to a continuous tension in life. When we are not actively engaged we feel this tension relaxed, but this feeling of relaxation is deceptive, for even then self-interest survives as may be within the experience of us all. Art relieves this inner strain also and we feel as if the burden of life has fallen from our shoulders. We forget ourselves and there instantly springs up happiness, for self-forgetfulness is the very essence of true happiness. Thus the aim of poetry, as that of other fine arts, is to induce in us a mood of detachment, albeit temporarily, and enable us to escape from the bonds of interested life.

'VISION OF VĀSAVADATTĀ'

Bhāsa was one of the earliest dramatists of India, but it is not known when exactly he flourished. All that is certain is that he lived long before Kālidāsa, for that poet refers to him as a 'far-famed' predecessor of his in the art of dramatic composition, and speaks of his works as 'ancient'. Though once renowned, Bhāsa had been all but forgotten till a few years ago when more than a dozen anonymous plays were published at Trivandrum and identified by their editor as the productions of this old dramatist. Some scholars have doubted the authenticity of these plays; and the evidence either way being unconvincing, the problem of their authorship should be regarded as still unsolved. What seems probable is that the plays do not represent the actual work of Bhāsa, but are only abridgments or adaptations made in later times by the actors of Malabar to meet the requirements of the local stage. The *Svapna-vāsavadatta* whose story is narrated below has long been recognized as the best of Bhāsa's plays. Thus a writer of the ninth century A.D. says that when the whole cycle of Bhāsa's plays was thrown into the fire, the *Svapna-vāsavadatta* alone remained unconsumed by the flames—a statement which in all likelihood signifies that the severest criticism could do no harm to it. Its chief excellences are the simplicity and directness of its style and the beauty and nobility of the life it depicts. The plot is drawn from the legendary lore of ancient India and relates to the life and doings of the half-mythical and half-historical hero, Udayana, who is said to have reigned over the province of Vatsa with its capital at Kauśāmbī, somewhere near modern Allahabad. The adventures of Udayana have furnished the theme for many a Sanskrit work, and the place which they have gained in Indian literature is next in importance only to that of the achievements of the heroes of the two great epics—the *Rāmāyaṇa* and the *Mahābhārata*. Bhāsa himself has dramatised the earlier portion of Udayana's life in his *Pratijñāyaugandharāyaṇa* which is included in the Trivandrum collection.

PRINCIPAL DRAMATIS PERSONAE

Udayana—King of Vatsa.
Vāsavadattā—Queen.
Padmāvatī—Princess of Magadha.
Yaugandharāyaṇa—Prime Minister.
Rumaṇvān—Commander-in-Chief.
The Clown.
The Chamberlain.
A religious student.
Padmāvatī's Nurse.

Once upon a time, there ruled in Kauśāmbī, the capital of the Vatsa country, a royal family of great prowess descended from Arjuna of *Mahābhārata* fame. The most renowned prince of that line was Udayana who was not inferior in valour or magnanimity of soul to Arjuna himself. This prince was highly accomplished and was particularly famous for his skill in music and in elephant-hunting. It was his addiction to the latter that led him into captivity while yet he was very young. But we are not now concerned with this mis-adventure of his. It is sufficient to remember that at Ujjain whereto he was taken as captive he was required to teach playing on the *vīṇā* to Vāsavadattā, the beloved daughter of his captor Mahāsena, the Valiant. Udayana, charmed by the beauty of the princess, fell in love with her and she also was smitten with a like passion for him. Escaping from the captivity soon, he returned with his pupil, the princess, to his capital Kauśāmbī where he married her. The match was not unwelcome to Mahāsena at all. In fact his motive in capturing Udayana and employing him later as music-master to his daughter was that a natural affection might grow between them. But the prince had been too impatient in running away with Vāsavadattā. Prevented thus from witnessing with their own eyes their daughter united in happy wedlock to the youth of their choice, Mahāsena and his queen celebrated the marriage with the portraits of the bride and the bridegroom thereby deriving what little satisfaction they could. Udayana resumed sovereignty over his kingdom with Vāsavadattā as his queen and for some time the couple lived happily together. There was also peace and plenty in the land. But adversity again overtook him, for the larger part of his kingdom was subjugated by his enemy Āruṇi.

There was at that time another great kingdom more to the East, Magadha, with its capital at Rājagṛha. Its king had lately died leaving the kingdom to his son Darśaka. Darśaka had a sister named Padmāvatī who was of uncommon beauty and who, if what soothsayers had predicted was true, would one day become the queen of Udayana. Udayana had, as his chief minister, one Yaugandharāyaṇa by name who was known as much for his loyalty to his sovereign as for his cleverness in policies of state. When the minister whose whole intent now was to see supremacy restored to Udayana, came to know of the prediction about Padmāvatī, he made up his mind to secure her hand for his king; for, should she marry him, it would be easy to get back the lost kingdom with the aid of the king of Magadha. Any royal house in the country would have welcomed matrimonial alliance with the prince of Kauśāmbī. But there was one insuperable difficulty; Udayana had already married Vāsavadattā for whom he bore intense love and nobody durst propose to him to take another to his wife. Yaugandharāyaṇa, however, would not be daunted by anything; and he devised a plan to achieve his purpose taking into his confidence Vāsavadattā as well as Rumaṇvān, the commander-in-chief. What this plan was we shall presently see.

Udayana, after his defeat by Āruṇi, was staying with his queen at a place called Lāvāṇaka, on the eastern frontier of his kingdom. Yaugandharāyaṇa then arranged with the commander-in-chief that, on a day on which the king had gone a-hunting, the royal camp should be set fire to, and the false news circulated that Vāsavadattā had been burnt to death along with Yaugandharāyaṇa who attempted to save her life. This was accordingly done after Yaugandharāyaṇa and Vāsavadattā had left Lāvāṇaka. Udayana returned when his camp was almost in ashes; and, learning that both his beloved wife and his trusted minister had perished in the flames, greatly bewailed his destiny. He was on the point of throwing himself into the fire which was still blazing but was saved by the entreaties of Rumaṇvān and the other ministers. He, however, refused to be consoled and recalling some one or other of the countless associations of his departed queen, he fainted again and again but was each time with great difficulty revived. After he was a little calmed, he was taken away from there with a veiw to turn his thoughts as far as possible from Vāsavadattā.

Now Yaugandharāyaṇa, who had entrusted the burden of administration as well as the care of his master to his colleague, donned the garb of the ascetic, and set out eastwards towards Magadha with Vāsavadattā, also in disguise, feigning that he was a pilgrim from Ujjain and representing the young lady accompanying him as his sister whom her husband had deserted. On their journey they had to pass through dense and lonely forests and Vāsavadattā was subjected to much fatigue and many vexations, neither of which she as princess or as queen had ever known. Yaugandharāyaṇa had to comfort her often by pointing out how the wheel of Fortune turns and, in turning, lowers even the good, and by reassuring her of coming prosperity. As they approached Rājagṛha they saw, in the woods that skirted the capital, a great many people—rather an unusual sight in a place which bore on it all the signs of an abode of ascetic men and women. The fact was that after the death of the old king, his widowed queen, Darśaka's mother, had retired from the world and was in a hermitage there, practising penance. That was the day on which Padmāvati, the princess of Rājagṛha, had come to pay her respects to her mother and receive her blessings. Naturally all the royal paraphernalia had followed her which accounted for the presence of so large a crowd in a place which one would expect to be lonely and secluded. To mark her visit to the forest, the princess had ordered it to be proclaimed that she would confer on any person staying there whatsoever he might ask for. 'O Ye ascetic dwellers of the forest! Listen, Listen, revered sirs! Her Royal Highness, the princess of Magadha, returning your love by hers, offers you as presents whatever you may choose. Who needs vessels? Who, clothes? And who that has duly completed his religious study seeks to pay the preceptor's fee? The princess in her devotion to virtue begs this favour of you—to tell her what she should give. Whoever wants anything may ask for it. To whom should she give? And what?' Yaugandharāyaṇa who had just arrived there with Vāsavadattā, when he heard this proclamation, thought he should seize the opportunity. He went up straight to the royal officer and desired to know if the princess would graciously take under her protection his sister till he returned from the pilgrimage which he pretended he had undertaken. Vāsavadattā was greatly perplexed when she saw the new turn events were taking; but she kept quiet as she fully confided in the wisdom and goodness of Yaugandharāyaṇa. Besides, her love for Udayana was so deep that she deemed no hardship was too great to bear for his sake. The prayer of Yaugandharāyaṇa was in one sense simple and it would be easy to grant it, especially for a princess like Padmāvatī. But in another sense, it was most embarrassing to comply with, for it meant looking after a young and beautiful woman of good family in the absence of all her relations. 'Your Royal Highness,' said the chief of her staff, 'the request is a big one. How can we agree to grant it? Easy would it be to give away money, life, penance: or, for that matter anything whatsoever; but hard it is to be surety for such a charge'. But the princess had given her word and would not retract it. 'Sir' said she, 'to proclaim first that anything that was desired would be given and then to hesitate to give is not right. What he says, should be done.' So Padmāvatī received Vāsavadattā, whose very appearance showed that she was a high-born lady that had seen better days; and it so happened that at the first meeting itself, they two began to like each other. Vāsavadattā, who had heard that Mahāsena, her father, was desiring the princess for his daughter-in-law, felt towards Padmāvatī like an elder sister; and Padmāvatī in her nobility of heart began to love and respect Vāsavadattā as her senior.

Just after Padmāvatī had plighted her word to Yaugandharāyaṇa for the care of Vāsavadattā, a religious student from Lāvāṇaka arrived there and he recounted how his study had been interrupted suddenly by a disastrous fire which, as he said, had not only killed the queen but, owing to the subsequent departure from there of the king, had rendered the place quite desolate. The vivid account which he gave of the lamentations of Udayana for his lost queen made a deep impression upon Padmāvatī; and she admired the prince so much for his tenderness and passion that love for him might be said to have stolen into her maiden heart then. After bidding adieu to them, the student pursued his way, and Yaugandharāyaṇa also proceeded on his journey, the secret aim of which was to carry through the rest of his scheme for re-installing his master on his ancestral throne. The two princesses also reached in due course the palace at Rājagṛha. Though sore at heart owing to separation from her lord, Vāsavadattā appeared outwardly happy in the company of Padmāvatī; and being very discreet, she gave not the slightest clue to her identity during all her long stay there.

To return to Udayana: The loss of his beloved queen had made life meaningless to him. Yet nobody could suggest to him the idea of marrying again. The very thought was unbearable to him. But time had its healing influence and once when he was on a political visit at Darśaka's court, the entreaties of the bride's people induced him at last to consent to his marriage with Padmāvatī. Vāsavadattā, as we know, all along believed that her own brother, the prince of Ujjain, was suitor for Padmāvatī's hand, and the news that she was engaged to marry Udayana was only casually made known to her. It happened thus: Once when Padmāvatī was indulging in some merry sport as became her maidenhood, Vāsavadattā said to her: 'You will, I know, be the daughter-in-law of Mahāsena's queen.' Padmāvatī asked her: 'Who is Mahāsena?' and then the following conversation took place:

Vāsavadattā: There is one Pradyota, king of Ujjain who is called 'Mahāsena' on account of his large and mighty army.

Padmāvatī's Nurse: The Princess does not like to wed his son.

Vāsavadattā: Whom else does she like then?

Nurse: There is Udayana, king of Vatsa. The princess admires him much.

Vāsavadattā: (*To herself*) So she wants to marry my lord. (*Aloud*) Why?

Nurse: Because of his great tenderness of heart.

Vāsavadattā: (*To herself*) I see, I see, even so was it with me.

Nurse: Princess, suppose he is ugly?

Vāsavadattā: No, no, he is quite handsome.

Padmāvatī: Friend, how do you know it?

Vāsavadattā: (*To herself*) My partiality for my lord has made me forget my resolve. What shall I do now? Yes, I see. (*Aloud*) Sister, thus the people of Ujjain say.

Padmāvatī: That is likely. He is not a stranger to Ujjain; and beauty, as they say, is a joy for all.

Though this incident reassured Vāsavadattā that her lord was alive and well, and was so far a source of great relief, her feeling had another side which made her quite sad. Yet so strong of heart was she that she did not, even under such trying circumstances, reveal her identity.

The wedding was soon arranged to take place at Rājagṛha, and when the bridal day arrived, Vāsavadattā herself, as Fate would have it, had to string the wedding garland which according to custom had to be entrusted to auspicious hands. She was chosen, in particular, because of her high rank and her friendship for the bride, not merely for her skill in such work. When the marriage was over, Udayana remained at Rājagṛha for some time. Vāsavadattā who was sorely distressed at the course which events had taken, would gladly have put an end to her life; but the hope that she might catch a glimpse of her sweet lord kept her alive. Now Padmāvatī had reared a beautiful flower-plant in the royal garden and it blossomed unusually well that season. Desirous of showing it to Udayana, she invited him to visit the garden; and herself, accompanied by Vāsavadattā, went there early to await his arrival. When the two friends had seen and admired the wealth of flowers which the plant had borne, Vāsavadattā asked 'Sister, how do you like your husband?' to which Padmāvatī replied: 'Friend, I do not know what to say; but I cannot bear to be away from him'. This made Vāsavadattā introspective and she was saying to herself 'Even Padmāvatī, who is but newly wedded to him feels thus! But I am yet alive!' when Padmāvatī interposed: 'I have however one doubt,' and added 'Was his Majesty as dear to Vāsavadattā as he is to me?' Vāsavadattā answered unawares—'Even more.' Padmāvatī at once asked 'How do you know?'

Vāsavadattā realized her mistake but it was too late and so added—'If she had not loved him so much, she would not have stolen out of her father's house to follow him.' At this stage Padmāvatī's nurse who also was there, intervening asked the princess, 'Why do you not, on a fit occasion, ask your lord to teach you how to play on the *vīṇā?*' Padmāvatī replied 'I have already done so.' Vāsavadattā then eagerly enquired—'And what was his reply?' and Padmāvatī said 'Without uttering a syllable, he fetched a deep sigh and kept quiet.' It was certain from this that Udayana, recollecting the excellent qualities of Vāsavadattā, was about to weep but restrained his tears out of regard for Padmāvatī's feelings. When Udayana arrived with the Vidūṣaka in the garden, Vāsavadattā, as was the custom, retired into a bower nearby, Padmāvatī also accompanying her; and from there the hapless lady looked upon her lord for the first time after her long separation. The conversation between him and his friend the Vidūṣaka, made it clear to her how devoted to her memory the king was. All this, though consoling in one way, brought tears to her eyes, but under the pretext of not disturbing Padmāvatī from keeping company with Udayana, she returned to her apartment in the palace.

One day, after this incident, Padmāvatī became ill, and when the news reached Udayana, he felt very uneasy; for, as the poet says, overmuch love always apprehends evil. He went to see his queen along with the Vidūṣaka to the garden-house where Padmāvatī was reported to be. But he did not find her, though the bed prepared for her was there. Expecting her soon, Udayana remained there and the Vidūṣaka, in order to while away time, began to narrate a story. The story was about Ujjain which at once put Udayana in mind of Vāsavadattā. Observing the effect which it had on the king, the Vidūṣaka changed the theme of his story. By that time Udayana fell asleep. The night was then growing cold; and the Vidūṣaka departed to fetch a *shawl* leaving the king alone, who began to talk of Vāsavadattā in his dream. At that time, Vāsavadattā who also had heard of her friend's indisposition which, because it meant anxiety to her lord, was doubly disconcerting to her, came to the garden-house to see her. When she came, she saw Udayana lying there on the couch; and mistaking him for Padmāvatī sat by his side. Just then Udayana said: 'O Vāsavadattā, why have you not had your toilet?' Vāsavadattā then discovered that it was not Padmāvatī but Udayana. While she was afraid that she had probably been discovered, Udayana muttered something from which she concluded that he was but dreaming. She accordingly made bold to stay there for sometime longer in order to have the satisfaction of looking well upon her lord. Udayana went on speaking in his dream; and Vāsavadattā taking up the conversation gave answers to his dream questions:

Udayana: Ah! Dear! Ah! Dear pupil! Why don't you speak to me?

Vāsavadattā: Speak? Dear! I *am* speaking.

Udayana: Are you angry with me?

Vāsavadattā: No, No, sad rather.

Udayana: If you are not angry, why are you not wearing your ornaments?

Vāsavadattā: Could there be any ornament better than being honoured thus by your love?

Udayana: Are you thinking of the separation?

Vāsavadattā: (*Angrily*) Away! Talk of separation even now?

Udayana: Then I shall appease you for having deserted you. (*Stretches forth both hands*).

Fearing that her stay there longer might upset all Yaugandharāyaṇa's plans, she resolved to leave the room; but, before doing so, she lifted up Udayana's arm which was then hanging down and placed it on the couch. That act half awoke Udayana. Realizing the situation, Vāsavadattā, though loath to part, left immediately; and Udayana followed her half-dreaming, but coming against the door-way, suddenly stopped. That awoke him fully but it was only after Vāsavadattā had made good her escape. Udayana saw a love-lorn form flit across, but was scarcely able to say whether what he had seen in that flash between waking and dream was actually Vāsavadattā or only a vision of her. When after some time the Vidūṣaka returned, Udayana, who was still thrilling with emotion, told him that he had encountered Vāsavadattā alive; but, as might be expected, the Vidūṣaka laughed at him saying that it should have been either a dream or a delusion. To which Udayana replied: 'If it be a dream, it is happy not to wake from it; or if it be a delusion, let me throughout be so deluded'. The incident only made his grief for the lost queen all the more poignant.

About this time Udayana had to leave Rājagṛha as the arrangements for the expedition against Āruṇi were complete, thanks chiefly to the untiring exertions of Yaugandharāyaṇa. Placing himself at the head of the allied armies of Vatsa and Magadha, he marched against the enemy and easily vanquished him. One day, after his victorious return, while Udayana was in an upstair hall of the royal mansion that had been set apart for him at Rājagṛha, he heard sweet music played by a street mendicant; and he at once discovered that the notes were emanating from the *vīṇā* which he had presented to his beloved Vāsavadattā,—so delicate was his perception of sound and so attached was he to Vāsavadattā. We have referred above to Udayana's captivity at Ujjain which led to his marriage with Vāsavadattā. It was with the romantic circumstances of that marriage that the *Ghoṣavatī*—for that was the name of the *vīṇā*—was associated and it was the very same instrument on which some one was playing in the street. Udayana at once made enquiries of the mendicant who revealed where and how he had secured it and in what plight it was when he saw it. It had been thrown upon brambles in a forest and it bore on its body the droppings of the winged folk of the forest. Udayana took the *vīṇā* which the minstrel willingly made over to him and it once again brought vividly before his mind the whole tragedy of Vāsavadattā; but it also helped him to spend his days closer, as it seemed to him, to his beloved lost.

Now Vāsavadattā's parents at Ujjain who had received the news of the restoration to Udayana of his lost kingdom, though sorrowing for the woeful loss of their daughter, sent envoys to congratulate him. They also sent, to serve as a sort of memento to him, the portraits of himself and Vāsavadattā which they had used in the marriage they celebrated after his escape from Ujjain. The envoys were admitted into the presence of Udayana, when Padmāvatī also was with him. After the usual exchange of courtesies, the portraits were presented and when Padmāvatī was about to bow to the likeness of her departed sister, she at once observed the resemblance of the person portrayed there as Vāsavadattā to the lady under her protection. When she mentioned this surprising resemblance to Udayana, he naturally grew anxious to see the lady but restrained himself when he learnt the circumstances in which she had come to be with Padmāvatī. Meanwhile Yaugandharāyaṇa also was there under the pretext of taking back his sister, and when the lady was sent for in response to his call, the identity of Vāsavadattā was at once made known. Yaugandharāyaṇa also revealed himself and, though he was conscious that he had striven all along for nothing but what was good for the king, explained with a quivering heart the circumstances which had prompted him to put this plan in operation. He implored the pardon of his sovereign for having separated his beloved queen from him for so long. The king thanked him after fully forgiving him and the party rejoiced very much indeed at the recovery of Vāsavadattā which had so beautifully synchronised with the restoration to Udayana of full sovereignty over his kingdom. Vāsavadattā's friendship for Padmāvatī was already old and firm; and so noble and generous was Pādmavatī herself that the knowledge that she had a rival in her did not in the least unsettle her mind. When it was suggested that the happy tidings should be communicated to the parents of Vāsavadattā at Ujjain, Udayana said he would himself repair thereto with all; and so he did to the infinite joy of Mahāsena and his queen.

The next noticeable feature in Kālidāsa is his vast learning. That he wrote in a language which had long ceased to be spoken is in itself a sufficient proof of this; but there are other evidences as well in support of this conclusion. The *formal* comparisons of which not a few are met with in his works (*vide*, e.g., *Raghuvaṁśa*, xv. 7) can be accounted for only by his superabundant learning. He was well-versed in the *Alaṁkāra*, *Nīti*, *Artha*, *Mīmāṁsā* and *Vyākaraṇa Śāstras*, his proficiency in the last being particularly noticeable. Even for a writer in a dead language, his style is remarkably correct, and in all his long poems there is scarcely any violation of Pāṇini's rules. A still more prominent feature of his learning is his thorough acquaintance with the *Purāṇas*. He is steeped in legendary lore and we may well take him to be the best representative of what is known as the *Purāṇic* age. Not only in the selection of subjects for his poems, but throughout his works, the poet shows his deep knowledge and appreciation of the divine and heroic myths of India. So true is this that a reader who cannot appreciate these myths will miss half the charm of Kālidāsa's poetry.

The question of Kālidāsa's learning naturally leads us to a consideration of his religious belief. As may be expected, Kālidāsa is a poet of faith. He believes in a definite and coherent system of doctrines and consequently no form of doubt appears anywhere in his works. The words which he puts into the mouth of Duṣyanta at the end of his immortal play of *Śākuntala*—probably his last work—may fitly be taken to furnish us with the key-note of his belief. While wishing well for his country and praying for the prosperity of the learned, Duṣyanta desires for *himself*, nothing but emancipation from re-birth. In the face of the brimming romanticism of Kālidāsa's poetry, it would be wrong to infer from this passage, that he was a pessimist. Such sentiments, as those referred to just now, only indicate what touch of seriousness there was in his life. He was not a pessimist, but was rather of that type of character, we find described in Tennyson's *Grandmother*—

> And happy has been my life, but I would not live it again.

Our poet has a strong faith in what is a constant element in all phases of Hindu religion—the law of *Karma*. Man may by virtue of his good deeds rise to the rank of the gods or by evil actions sink to the level of the lower beings; but his final aim ought to be to escape from the trammels of re-birth, whether high or low.

Kālidāsa believes in the ultimate existence of one Supreme Being from which the universe emanates and into which it is finally absorbed. This Being, Kālidāsa terms, in agreement with the teaching of the Upaniṣads, almighty, absolute, omniscient and omnipresent. For the purposes of evolving the world the highest Being differentiates itself into the three gods of the Hindu Trinity. Kālidāsa states, with a tolerance characteristic of him, that all these gods are of equal rank, and that a believer may select for special worship whichever of the three forms appeals to him most. Though this form of monotheism—for it is not *advaitism* in the sense which that word has acquired since Śaṁkara's time—was the professed religion of our poet, the special cult to which he adhered in daily life was *Śaivism*. The *Śaivic* colour of his faith may have arisen from the accident of the age in which he was born or of the family to which he belonged. In the reply given by Pārvatī to the ascetic who questions the propriety of her selecting *Śiva* for her consort (*Kumārasaṁbhava*, v), Kālidāsa, we may imagine, explains his own special attachment to this form of the godhead. The close acquaintance which the poet shows with the customs and beliefs of the highest Aryan society, the readiness and naturalness with which he refers to Brahminic ritual and the general tenor of his writings indicate that he was in all probability a Brahmin. The commonly current notions that he was a shepherd and so forth must thus be attributed to that tendency in man by which he readily invents circumstances that add to the glory of the person whom he decides to admire.

KĀLIDĀSA THE POET

Poetry is of sentiment as well as of diction, and while the special merit of many writers lies in one or the other of these, a few excel in both. Kālidāsa is of the latter type and his poetry appeals to us as much by the elegance of its form as by the power of its ideas. Perfect artist as he is, Kālidāsa avoids extravagance of all kinds. There is nothing like pomp in his manner and he nowhere succumbs to that tendency to 'over-exaggerate' (*atyukti*) which spoils so much of Sanskrit poetry. His conceptions are natural, though bold; his similes are proverbially apt; and his epithets are always fully suggestive. In propriety of dialogue and sentiment he is unsurpassed. More striking than all these, is his strong love for Nature. He looks upon things in Nature with a peculiarly tender feeling, and we may regard him as another St. Francis of Assissi, calling the very flowers his sisters and mothers, and 'looking upon the hill with tenderness and making dear friendship with the streams and groves'. His descriptions of Nature are everywhere tinged with this family love and with such descriptions he combines profound interpretation of human life and character.

One more point that we may notice here is that Kālidāsa, as has been remarked by a discerning critic, is a 'poet of love.' Love forms the prevailing sentiment of all his plays and it furnishes the *motif* to his *Meghasandeśa*—one of the most exquisite of lyrics. In his other works also, the poet shows a partiality for this sentiment. But we should remember that love as portrayed by Kālidāsa is different from that described in much of later Sanskrit poetry. As the latter is mostly sensual in its character, the word *śṛṅgāra* (love) has come to be associated in this, its perverted sense, with Sanskrit literature in general. This is very unfortunate, for the sentiment of love as delineated by the earlier poets, especially Kālidāsa, is of a pure type and has the least to do with the love of the flesh. Even this higher love appears in two phases in Sanskrit literature—one of them corresponding to the Hindu idea of *pravṛtti* or 'activity', and the other to that of *nivṛtti* or 'withdrawal'. The former recognises love (*kāma*) as one of the three aims in life (*trigaṇa*), the other two being *artha* and *dharma*. According to this conception of life, wisdom consists in following all the above aims with equal devotion, and making life a harmonious whole. Although such an ideal makes for social order and individual purity, it can scarcely be described as the highest, for it is not wholly spiritual in character. The second ideal of *nivṛtti*, on the other hand, merges the immediate in the ultimate and recognises *mokṣa* as the *sole* end in life (*parama-puruṣārtha*). According to this ideal, man should not rest satisfied with a mere harmonising of the various temporal aims of life, but should, from the very beginning, endeavour to set free the universal in him from the limits of individuality. Viewed in this light, love acquires a new significance. True love is not what can take a circumspect view of all that concerns the self, but that which would sacrifice that very self for the sake of the object loved. Love thus casts off self-love and becomes but another form of the love of the Yogin for the universe with which he feels his kinship (*Īśā Up. 6*)—but another means of realizing unity by breaking through the bonds of selfishness. It is love in this highest sense that we find in Kālidāsa and to him belongs the credit of having given the best poetic expression to this ancient Hindu ideal of love and life.

THE VOCABULARY OF THE 'MEGHA-SANDEŚA'

This is an alphabetical list of the words found in the *Megha-sandeśa* of Kālidāsa; and, although it does not cite the actual passages in which the several words occur, it gives complete references to the places in the poem where they do. The Swamiji, who has compiled it, is now engaged in preparing similar lists for the remaining poems and plays of the same poet.

A concordance of this kind may serve several useful purposes. Its utility to the lexicographer, for instance, who is intent on giving illustrative quotations from standard authors is obvious. In the case of a work like the *Ṛigveda* containing obscure terms, it helps to determine their meanings through a comparison of their uses in different contexts. Its main use here will be in the study of the poet's style on its formal side. By glancing over this list, we can see the supreme simplicity of his vocabulary. There is nothing that is archaic or abstruse in it; and it is also singularly free from out-of-the-way derivatives and ponderous compounds, which may easily disfigure the composition of a poet writing in a learned language like Sanskrit. It shows, by the way, that the highest form of poetry can be fashioned out of the simplest words. The range of the vocabulary again is surprisingly wide, considering the short compass of the poem. To mention only one other striking feature: Very few words and phrases are used in the work more than twice, and several appear only once. In the *Ṛtu-saṁhāra*, for example, (assuming that it is by Kālidāsa) recurrent expressions which serve no special poetic purpose are not at all uncommon; and one may safely conclude on the ground merely of this feature of the style that the present work is later, even though there were no other indications of it. When similar concordances relating to the remaining works of the poet which are all much longer are published, they are sure to disclose other characteristic excellences of his style and also throw further light on the course of its development. Meanwhile those who are devoted to the muse of Kālidāsa will feel grateful to the Swamiji for this new aid to the study and appreciation of a poem which may, without exaggeration, be described as one of the greatest and finest lyrics in the language.

Dramatis Personae

Mādhava	Hero, son of minister Devarāta.
Mālatī	Heroine, daughter of minister Bhūrivasu.
Makaranda	A friend of Mādhava.
Kalahaṁsa	Mādhava's attendant.
Nandana	Companion of Bhūrivasu's royal master.
Kāmandakī	A Buddhistic nun.
Avalokitā and Saudāmanī	Her pupils.
Mandārikā	Kalahaṁsa's sweetheart.
Lavaṅgikā	Mālatī's nurse.
Madayantikā	Nandana's sister.
Aghoraghaṇṭa	A fanatic devotee of Kālī.
Kapālakuṇḍalā	His pupil.

Devarāta and Bhūrivasu were two ministers of state—one employed in Vidarbha and the other in another kingdom whose capital was Padmāvatī. They were great friends in youth when they pursued their studies together; and before they parted, they had vowed to bring about matrimonial alliance between their children, if ever they should become fathers. There was born of Devarāta in course of time a son; and of Bhūrivasu, a daughter: the veriest jewels among children. The boy was named Mādhava; and the girl, Mālatī. As Mādhava grew up and was fit to go out to learn, his father sent him to Padmāvatī. In selecting that place for study, Devarāta had the idea that Mādhava's presence there might put his old friend in mind of the bridal compact, if he chanced to forget it. He also thought that the great personal charm of the youth and the qualities of his mind would serve as an inducement to Bhūrivasu to offer Mālatī in marriage to him. Bhūrivasu had not at all forgotten the school-day compact and the youthful couple would readily have been united in happy wedlock; but there was one formidable obstacle. The king of Padmāvatī had a boon companion by name Nandana, who was neither young nor handsome; and he was seeking the hand of Mālatī through the king. Bhūrivasu was in a fix. He could not agree to such an ill-assorted match; nor could he openly refuse to give the girl in marriage to one that was the favourite of his royal master. When the king once actually broached the matter, he thought it best to give an inoffensive but equivocal reply. There was then at Padmāvatī a Buddhistic nun, Kāmandakī, who was a great friend of both Devarāta and Bhūrivasu. In fact it was in her presence that they in their student days had plighted their word to see their children married. She had also known and fondled Mālatī from her infancy, and was therefore as much interested as the girl's parents themselves in seeing her united to so worthy a youth as Mādhava. Kāmandakī was besides very clever; and her position as a nun gave her an advantage which a secular official like Bhūrivasu could not well command. Bhūrivasu, who knew the friendship which Kāmandakī bore him, entrusted the whole affair to her and remained unconcerned to all outward appearance. Kāmandakī on her part was not unwilling, though a nun, to undertake a good office of that sort —especially as she felt whenever she thought of the equal excellence of Mālatī and Mādhava that they were almost predestined to wed each other.

Now it so happened that Mālatī was one day standing at an upper casement of her father's mansion as Mādhava passed along the road below. She saw him, and seeing in her case was loving. This love at first sight deepened as she watched him passing not unoften the same way. It soon became known to her attendants that she was in love and that Mādhava was her sweetheart. Kāmandakī wanted first to see that the two young people fell in love with each other before she actively exerted herself to bring about their union. Half of her wish had now been fulfilled; and the other half also was soon accomplished by the cleverness of one of her pupils, Avalokitā. It was the spring season and the custom for youthful maidens then was to go to the Garden of Love outside the city to pay their adoration to Cupid there in the shrine dedicated to that deity. Avalokitā, who knew that Mālatī would also follow the custom, arranged that Mādhava should be present in the garden at the time. He went there alone. But seeing a *vakula* tree in full blossom approached it; and discovering a wealth of flowers adorning the ground beneath, he in a holiday mood picked up the new-fallen flowers and began to string them into a garland of exquisite design. He had not yet reached to the end of his task when Mālatī who had been worshipping inside the shrine came out. As Mādhava saw her graceful form, he fell in love with her as quickly as she had done with him before. The sight so much distracted him that though he continued making the garland, it left visible traces on his workmanship. Mālatī also came up to the tree with her attendants, attracted by the flowers; and as she neared the spot where Mādhava stood, she saw him more closely than she had ever done before. Her attendants noticing a sudden change in her demeanour and recognizing Mādhava in the youth that was there, first exchanged smiles with one another and then jestingly drew their mistress's attention towards him. Mādhava, as he saw her, espied marks of love already deep-rooted in her though he could not guess who the fortunate youth was that had been the object of her interest. Soon after Mālatī, mounting a stately elephant that had been waiting for her, left the garden for her home, but not without casting back glances in the direction of Mādhava. He noticed this sign of love for him, although he hesitated to draw much hope from it. A little later Mālatī's nurse, Lavaṅgikā, returned to the place under the pretext of collecting the *vakula* flowers and told him how very much her mistress admired the garland which he was making. Mādhava replied that he deemed it his great good fortune that it had evoked the admiration of so noble and beautiful a damsel; and, taking the garland from off his neck, gave it to Lavaṅgikā. From her, he learnt that the maiden that had stolen his heart when he was feeling all helpless in her presence was no other than Mālatī, the daughter of the minister, Bhūrivasu, his father's friend.

Mādhava stood there till he could no longer see the form of Mālatī. When she disappeared from his sight, he turned back only to discover that what had filled him with joy but a moment ago had become a source of intense anguish to his heart. He left the place after some time and was returning slowly, dwelling on his new passion, when he met his bosom friend, Makaranda, advancing towards him. They both sat down in an arbour there. Surprised to find the change that had suddenly come over Mādhava, Makaranda inquired of him as to its cause. After great pressure from him, Mādhava opened his heart to his friend and told him how he had met Mālatī that morning and what all had happened. Makaranda, when he learnt how love-forlorn Mālatī seemed and with what eagerness she looked at Mādhava, assured him that she was in love with him; for virtue, as he said, is incapable of inconstancy and maidens like Mālatī will not allow their eyes to stray from the path which their hearts have once taken. When Makaranda was giving other reasons to think so, Mādhava's attendant Kalahaṁsa, who had for some time been in the same part of the garden and had overheard all that had passed between the two freinds, presented himself saying 'This also', and handed over to Makaranda, a portrait of his master. Pining with love for Mādhava, Mālatī had once put on canvas his likeness; and it was that very likeness that Kalahaṁsa had obtained through his beloved Mandārikā and brought here now. It helped greatly to confirm what Makaranda had thought was probable and what Mādhava's own heart was persuading him to believe ever since he had seen Mālatī. Now Makaranda who had not met Mālatī but had just heard so much about her beauty and dignity suggested to his friend that he might paint her portrait on the same canvas so that he might delight his eyes by looking at it. Mādhava consented; and not only did he paint her likeness there but also added the following couplet:

> 'Whatever lovely things in life there be,
> Sole joy thou art to me, O Mālatī.'

Observing the two forms, Makaranda admired their mutual fitness and foretold that where God and Cupid had planned alike, nothing would go amiss. At that stage, Mandārikā, who as we know was instrumental in bringing away the portrait, came pursuing Kalahaṁsa and demanded it of him. When she got it and discovered it improved in the manner mentioned, she pretended to be angry but inwardly felt glad that it would advance the cause that was so dear to the heart of Bhūrivasu. From her, Mādhava learnt how and when Mālatī had first seen him, and how deep her attachment for him was. Mandārikā went away taking the portrait with her. Mādhava and Makaranda also left the garden as the sun by then had reached the zenith.

These incidents were soon made known to Kāmandakī who was glad that the mutual love between Mālatī and Mādhava to which she was looking forward had become a matter of fact, and she went to meet Mālatī the same afternoon. She was at that time alone with Lavaṅgikā, the subject of their conversation naturally being Mādhava:

Mālatī: And what happened then, friend?

Lavaṅgikā: Then the high-souled youth gave me the garland. (*Hands it over to Mālatī*).

Mālatī: (*Receiving it and looking at it joyfully*) It is unevenly strung in one portion.

Lavaṅgikā: You yourself are to blame for it.

Mālatī: How?

Lavaṅgikā: Because he was then so much taken off his mind by you.

Mālatī: Friend Lavaṅgikā, you seem to have made up your mind to comfort me under all circumstances.

Lavaṅgikā: Have I not told you that I saw with my own eyes clear signs of love in him?

Mālatī: Could it all be natural to him and we are deceived? Or is it as you guess?

Lavaṅgikā: (*Ironically*) Your deportment then, I suppose, was also natural!

Mālatī: (*Bashfully*) And then?

Lavaṅgikā: I returned and on my way went to Mandārikā with whom I had left the portrait in the morning.

Mālatī: With what intent?

Lavaṅgikā: You know she is in love with Kalahaṁsa. I thought she would show it to him and bring good news.

Mālatī: (*To herself*) Could he have shown the portrait to his master? (*To Lavaṅgikā*) And what is the good news she has brought?

Lavaṅgikā: Here is the portrait and you see from it what solace Mādhava should have derived from it. (*Shows the portrait to her*).

Mālatī: (*Contemplating it*) Alas! Even now my heart feels not sure. It despairs where it ought to hope. Oh! I see something written here. (*Reads it.*) Illustrious youth, your words are not less sweet than your form. But alas! your sight, though so joyful then, has become a torment to me since. Lucky are those damsels that never meet you; or having met, are yet able to be mistresses over their hearts.

At this stage Kāmandakī stepped in accompanied by Avalokitā; and in the conversation that followed, she artfully let fall the news that Mālatī was being sought by the king for his favourite Nandana and that Bhūrivasu was likely to agree. The mention of this unwelcome suitor sent a dart, as it were, to the heart of Mālatī; and she wished she had not been born. Kāmandakī did not disclose her intention to thwart, if possible, Nandana's purpose; but she gave general advice which suggested that the choice of a husband against the will of the elders in such circumstances was not without precedent in the history of virtuous maidens. Just then Avalokitā reminded her of Mādhava's indisposition, news of which had reached them before; and it gave occasion for Mālatī to learn that the youth on whom she had set her heart was the son of the much-esteemed Devarāta, her father's great friend. His high birth recommended Mādhava to her affections the more and it was a joy to her to find that her heart had, by instinct, made the right choice.

On a certain day, Mālatī was to go to the temple of Śaṁkara outside the city and worship the God of all auspiciousness with flowers gathered by herself. When Kāmandakī learnt of this, she instructed Mādhava to be there at the time, with a view to bring about what may appear a casual interview between the two lovers. Kāmandakī also went there. Soon Mālatī arrived accompanied by Lavaṅgikā, bewailing her lot in life which had made Nandana her suitor and wondering if she would ever again have the joy of meeting Mādhava. After she had gathered flowers for the worship, Kāmandakī made her sit under a shady tree to rest from the fatigue. Then she spoke of the great merits of Mādhava and mentioned how his passion for Mālatī was preying upon him. Lavaṅgikā in her turn informed Kāmandakī of the similar affliction of her mistress owing to her love for Mādhava and showed her the picture she had painted as well as the *vakula* garland she was wearing concealed round her neck. While they were conversing thus to the great joy of Mādhava who remained unseen near by, and Mālatī was ardently listening, a sudden cry informed them that a ferocious tiger kept in the neighbouring garden had burst open the doors of its iron cage and attacked Madayantikā, sister of Nandana, the would-be bridegroom of Mālatī. The news greatly agitated the party; and Mādhava, leaving the place where he was, stepped into their midst creating agreeable surprise in Mālatī and himself feeling in her presence as if he were 'under a shower of heavenly ambrosia.' Soon it transpired that Makaranda who had learnt of Nandana's efforts and was hastening to be with Mādhava lest the unwelcome news should unsettle him too much, saw the pitiable state in which Madayantikā was and went to her rescue. Makaranda was injured in his encounter with the tiger but he succeeded in slaying the animal and saving Madayantikā from its fury. When Kāmandakī and the rest went out, they saw Makaranda had fainted and was being supported by Madayantikā. Seeing his friend in that sad condition, Mādhava also swooned. After some time both the friends recovered, the one with Madayantikā's ministrations and the other with Mālatī's loving caresses. The incident strengthened further the love between Mālatī and Mādhava. It also gave rise to a like affection between Makaranda and Madayantikā which betrayed itself through 'an intermingling of tremulous looks'. At this juncture, a messenger brought the news that the king had settled the marriage of Mālatī with Nandana; and Madayantikā left with him to congratulate her brother. The news from Nandana upset our hero who heard it for the first time now, and he cursed his fate which had planted in his heart such fruitless love. While Kāmandakī was asking him to be of good cheer, Bhūrivasu's wife sent word to her to fetch Mālatī immediately. She left the place and Mālatī followed her thinking that she was looking upon Mādhava for the last time. Mādhava also departed soon after along with Makaranda.

With all his hopes thus suddenly blighted, Mādhava felt that he could never more think of love for his matchless Mālatī. So in a desperate mood he went in the evening towards the graveyard to invoke the aid of the spirits of the dead. But what was his surprise when he heard the wailings of Mālatī there! Forgetting his errand of despair, he rushed in the direction from which the pitiful cry came, and reached the temple of Kālī. When he went in he saw a terrific votary of Kālī there, Aghoraghaṇṭa by name, standing with upraised sword and reciting a hymn. By his side stood a woman, Kapālakuṇḍalā, his pupil. There was seated before them Mālatī decked in all the symbols of a victim about to be sacrificed. When Mādhava saw her, she had the sweet syllables of his name on her lips which gave him one more proof of the secure place he had won in her heart.

the world of such a prince among youths. Thus will you fulfil your friend's last wishes.

Lavaṅgikā: May God avert all harm! I cannot bear to hear more of this.

Mālatī: Friend, dear is Mālatī's life to you, not Mālatī herself.

Lavaṅgikā: How do you mean?

Mālatī: You ask me to survive this shame. This is now my resolve; I have offended the saviour of my life by becoming another's; and I want to atone for it by ceasing to be. Don't you stand in my way. *(Falls at the feet of Lavaṅgikā.)*

Then Lavaṅgikā motioned to Mādhava who along with Makaranda stood concealed within the shrine; and he, taking Lavaṅgikā's place gently, went on answering the sad questions which Mālatī put. At last half-agreeing that she might do as she pleased, he begged for her last embrace. Poor Mālatī, least suspecting who had replaced Lavaṅgikā, rose with tearful eyes and threw herself into Mādhava's arms thanking him for his permission. She thought of giving her friend as a final present the dearest thing in her eyes—the *vakula* garland which she so much cherished ever since the day it had reached her. As she was trying to transfer it from her neck to that of her friend, she discovered whom she was addressing. Mādhava told her that she was too selfish in complaining of her own distress, ignoring his. At this time Kāmandakī came in; and, well pleased to find the time so propitious, betrothed Mālatī to Mādhava showering her choicest blessings upon them both.

Kāmandakī's plan compassed more than this betrothal. So she proposed that Makaranda should dress himself like Mālatī, wearing the clothes and putting on the ornaments presented by the king, to meet Nandana. When Makaranda accordingly appeared in Mālatī's attire before the party, he produced immense merriment. Kāmandakī and Lavaṅgikā departed immediately with this mock-Mālatī, leaving our hero and heroine behind in charge of Avalokitā. Makaranda played his new *role* so cleverly that the wedding with Nandana was celebrated, his identity being suspected by nobody. It was arranged that Mālatī should be taken to the bridegroom's residence in the evening.

But meanwhile Nandana, impatient of meeting his new bride, approached Makaranda in his usual vulgar manner, but was repulsed by him with disdain. Nandana was greatly offended. He had heard of Mālatī's love for Mādhava. Making that the plea for rejecting her, he left his supposed bride in great wrath. Kāmandakī had succeeded in creating a dislike for Mālatī in Nandana's mind, but the final success of her plan was yet far from sight, as the king's attitude in the matter had to be reckoned with. When the news of Mālatī's affront reached Madayantikā, she felt the insult to her brother as her own and resolved to see Mālatī and prevail upon her to agree to meet her brother in good humour. Madayantikā reached Bhūrivasu's residence with much indignation but as she entered Mālatī's apartment, Makaranda noticing her come pretended to be asleep. Madayantikā, unwilling to disturb him, seated herself on his couch and began to converse with Lavaṅgikā. After they had referred to the untoward incident that had enraged Nandana, their conversation turned upon Madayantikā's love for Makaranda, her great benefactor. As she confessed her deep love for him, Makaranda was greatly pleased to listen to it. On her being cunningly asked whether, if Makaranda met her that moment and proposed to marry her, she would yield her assent, she replied that he who had hazarded his life for her sake had entire liberty over her. Makaranda discovered himself then and Madayantikā having agreed to run away with her lover, they all started in the night for the garden where Mālati and Mādhava were. Soon after the city guards who had been apprised of the elopement, pursued the party and overtook them. Makaranda stayed behind to meet them while the others advanced towards the garden to inform Mādhava of all that had happened. Mādhava started at once to assist his friend. In the confusion that followed, Mālatī stepped out alone in anxiety to look for her lord. Just at that time, Kapālakuṇḍalā, who, as we know, had sworn revenge, came and carried Mālatī away. She had been waiting all along for a fit opportunity to perpetrate her misdeed unobserved by anybody. Such an opportunity had now arrived and she conveyed Mālatī to a hill known as Śrī-parvata 'to tear her to pieces there', as she said. Mādhava and Makaranda who had successfully routed the guards were conducted to the king. When he learnt of their prowess and of their high rank, he, with his usual partiality for merit, pardoned them. When the two youths returned to the garden soon after, they were sorely disappointed not to find Mālatī there and they immediately set out in search of her.

The first place in which they looked for her was Kāmandakī's residence. When they did not find her there, they grew suspicious and when further search was equally fruitless, they grew desperate and took her for lost. The grief of Mādhava knew no bounds. As he was unable to bear the sight of the things associated with Mālatī, Makaranda took him away to a wood skirting a hill some miles beyond the city, hoping that his friend might find some relief there. But it proved a change from bad to worse. Any and every sight in that pretty wood would unbalance his mind and it needed all the cleverness which Makaranda could command to see that he did not go mad over the loss of his love. One day when Mādhava fainted and lay in a death-like swoon, Makaranda, despairing of his recovery and feeling his own life a burden, made up his mind to drown himself in a river close by. But just at that time, an unfamiliar voice spoke to him asking him to forbear. Makaranda was more than surprised and looking up discovered an ascetic lady before him. She asked whether he was Makaranda and on his answering 'I am that hapless being', Saudāmanī—for that was her name—told him that she had news of Mālatī and showed him the *vakula* garland in support of what she said. Makaranda was overwhelmed with joy, and he dashed at once with Saudāmanī to where Mādhava was lying. Mādhava had just recovered his consciousness. They saw him first blaming the god of wind for bringing him back to consciousness from the swoon where he had found an escape from sorrow; and then begging the same god with bowed head and joined hands to waft his life to where Mālatī was or blow on something of her to him. At that time Saudāmanī placed the garland in his hands. Mādhava was overjoyed, and the holy woman disclosed how she had come by it. Śrī-parvata whereto Kapālakuṇḍalā had carried Mālatī away was the place where Saudāmanī performed penance. On hearing the screamings of Mālatī, Saudāmanī went to her help and after rescuing her from the clutches of Kapālakuṇḍalā, had hastened to convey the good news knowing that Mālatī was so dear to her former preceptor, Kāmandakī and to them all. Then suddenly Saudāmanī with her supernatural power disappeared taking away Mādhava with her. Makaranda who was left alone, not knowing what it might be and marvelling at the sport of fate as it seemed to him, resolved to go and report the whole matter to Kāmandakī. She and her friends, disgusted with the turn which affairs had taken in spite of their best efforts, had meanwhile repaired to the same wood,—there to fall from some precipice and kill themselves. As Makaranda was relating to them what had happened, there was an unexpected flash of splendour and Mādhava appeared with Mālatī restored to him, thus preventing the wholesale tragedy that would otherwise have been enacted there that day. Saudāmanī also had accompanied Mālatī and Mādhava; but, hearing on her way that Bhūrivasu, grieving over the loss of his daughter, was about to end his life, had gone thither to prevent that calamity. She had succeeded in turning back the sorrowing minister from his resolve by communicating to him in time the happy news of his daughter's safety. She soon returned to where Kāmandakī and the others were with a letter from the king, written in the presence of Nandana. The king, when apprised of everything, had written to Mādhava graciously approving of not only his marriage with Mālatī but also that of Makaranda with Madayantikā. Fate proved to be friendly to the two couples in the end; and Love, though it had taken a chequered course, was triumphant at last.

'UTTARA-RĀMACARITA'

We often assume that literary standards, to which the accidents of our generation have given currency, are of absolute value, and expect that all works, no matter when or where they were written, should conform to those standards. The assumption, however, is far from right. Every nation develops its own ideal of art, as it does its own ideal of life; and it would be quite unfair to judge a writer by standards of which he was not aware or which he perhaps deliberately set aside. It is, therefore, necessary before speaking about a work like the *Uttara-rāmacarita* to know exactly what the author's aim was in writing it. The theme of the highest Sanskrit poetry is human emotion, and the poet so represents it in his work as to arouse in us a kind of disinterested joy which is known as *rasa* and which, on account of its disinterestedness, may be described as spiritual in character. In experiencing this unique joy we forget ourselves, and feel, for the time being, as if elevated above the realities of everyday life. In other words, the Sanskrit poet furnishes us in his poetry with a form of spiritual diversion. That is his foremost aim, and he subordinates the whole technique of his art to its attainment. All other aims such as criticism of life, portraying of human character, inculcation of moral truths, etc.,—so far as they are recognized as aims at all—recede to the background. Keeping in mind this ideal of Sanskrit poetry, let us describe the *Uttara-rāmacarita* under the usual heads of plot, characterization and *rasa*.

PLOT

According to a well-known rule of Sanskrit literary criticism, the plot of a Nāṭaka—the chief variety of the Indian drama—must be familiar, and be either historical or legendary. The significance of this restriction on the choice of the subject is to avoid the distractions of a new and complex story. *Rasa* being the spirit and soul of a drama in common with other forms of poetry, the plot becomes merely its outer vesture, and it serves its purpose best when it thrusts itself least on the attention of the spectator. In fact, in a perfect drama we should not become conscious of the plot at all. Accordingly, Sanskrit poets look upon any obtrusion of the plot as a sort of materialism in poetry. The restriction, however, need not be viewed as a check on the exercise of inventive power by the poet; for although the story is to be familiar in its outline, the special situations which a dramatic composition requires may entirely be the creation of the author's genius, provided only the innovations introduced are necessitated by the chief aim of his art, viz., the development of *rasa*.

There are in the *Uttara-rāmacarita* some alterations in the story which, as is well-known, is taken from the last book of the *Rāmāyaṇa*. In the epic, when Lakṣmaṇa leaves Sītā near Vālmīki's hermitage and returns, the pupils of Vālmīki carry the news to him. The sage comes to meet the helpless queen and knowing, as he does, that she is pure and innocent, consoles her and takes her to his hermitage. There, later on, Sītā gives birth to Lava and Kuśa. But in the play, soon after the cruel decree of Rāma drives her to the seclusion of the forest, Sītā throws herself into the Ganges, and in the agony of the situation gives birth to the twins. Gaṅgā and Bhūmi intervene and lead her to their world, after entrusting the children to the care of Vālmīki. In the epic story it is known to almost all where Sītā is. Śatrughna, on his way to fight Lavaṇa, halts in Vālmīki's hermitage, and it is on that very day that Sītā is delivered of the twins. According to one recension of the *Rāmāyaṇa*, Śatrughna has even a talk with Sītā before he leaves the hermitage. Such knowledge of Sītā's place of residence would not aid the development of pathos so well as a total ignorance of her whereabouts. In the drama her fate is all unknown, and the resulting grief is proportionately great. Witness, for instance, the helpless misery of Rāma when he says to Vāsantī, in reply to her question as to what had become of Sītā in the forest—*kravyādbhir aṅgalatikā niyataṁ viluptā*. Again in the epic, Lava and Kuśa do not meet Rāma in the hermitage, but in the sacrificial hall at Ayodhyā, whereto they are sent by Vālmīki to recite his poem—the *Rāmāyaṇa*. Observing their features, Rāma strongly suspects that they are Sītā's children, and sends for Vālmīki. The sage appears with Sītā. Her innocence is established on supernatural evidence, and the people's doubts are removed. But Sītā prays to her mother to relieve her of the iniquities of life; the earth opens and receives her, and she disappears declaring her purity. In the play, on the other hand, she is restored to

Rāma—a change which gives a happy ending to the story, and is to be traced to the Indian aversion to a tragic close.

The above are the main deviations from the original story, but if we take the spirit into consideration, it has undergone a total transformation in the hands of the dramatist. For example, the incidents connected with Lavaṇa and Śambūka, and even the Aśvamedha sacrifice, stand by themselves in the epic. In the drama, on the other hand, they all blend with the main story, whereby complete unity of action is secured. Again, there are many situations invented by the poet, like the visit to the picture gallery in the first act or the introduction of an inset play in the last. The visit to the picture gallery, in particular, is very skilfully handled, and with its restrained touches and judicious selection of incidents aids at once the progress of the plot, the portraying of character, and the development of *rasa*.

CHARACTERIZATION

As we have already stated, the poet's thoughts are not primarily set on character-drawing and the situations he describes serve, in the first instance, a different purpose. But these very situations reveal the character of the persons appearing on the stage, and when it is a great poet we are considering, the characterization is vivid indeed. To be consistent with his ultimate aim, the poet does not, however, elaborate details. There are a few strokes, and they are clear and characteristic. Witness how beautifully Kālidāsa differentiates between Anasūyā and Priyaṁvadā, although they have so much in common.

Before dealing with individual characters appearing in our play, it is necessary to refer to a certain misconception in regard to the nature of the characters in a Sanskrit drama. Indian literary critics divide heroes and heroines into certain classes, and from this it is sometimes hastily concluded that the Sanskrit drama does not represent individuals, but only conventional and generalized types. There are two errors in thinking so. To begin with, this classification applies only to heroes and heroines, and not to the other characters. In the *Uttara-rāmacarita*, for example, there are many like Janaka and Lakṣmaṇa, who do not come under this classification and whom the poet depicts quite as individuals. Now as regards heroes and heroines also, it is essential to remember that types are not of necessity generalized. A generalized character is one that is devoid of all individual traits, but this charge cannot be brought against the characters that appear in a Sanskrit drama for they do exhibit special traits over and above what is common to their class. Thus, while Rāma and Duṣyanta are both of the *dhīrodātta* type, they, as represented by the dramatists, possess their own individuality and are unmistakably distinct.

The qualities which we ordinarily associate with Rāma—his magnanimity, his filial piety, his kindly disposition, etc.,—are all clearly revealed during the course of the play. He is not anywhere represented as a god; but his is a magnetic personality and to see him is to love him and revere him. A notable feature of his character is a high sense of duty. In him Bhavabhūti has given us a supreme example of a hero who realizes to the full what duty means, and what sacrifices it may demand of its votaries. Duty is commonly regarded as the opposite of pleasure, but often one duty conflicts with another, and problems of conflicting duties are the hardest to solve. To distinguish 'right' from 'wrong' is easy enough, but to differentiate 'ought' from 'right' is very difficult. Two calls come to Rāma and he finds himself in a moral dilemma. He has not merely to sacrifice his pleasure, but also to forget his duty to Sītā, whom he knows to be so good and great and who has, for his sake, already undergone so much suffering. When Rāma once realizes that the people's suspicion, although not correct, is justifiable, and that there is no means within human reach to convince them of Sītā's innocence, he decides to exile her. That is his duty as a king, and he is first a king and then Rāma. Yet Rāma's grief for Sītā cannot be greater; nor his faith in her deeper. This sternness of duty is the main moral lesson which Bhavabhūti wishes us to learn from the play—so far as a poet can be said to do that at all; for duty furnishes the keynote to the character of more than one personage whom he brings on the stage, e.g., Janaka, Candraketu, Durmukha. In all this, however, Bhavabhūti's picture of Rāma is at one with Vālmīki's picture of him. But in one respect the Rāma of the play is very different from the Rāma of the epic. The latter, although deeply grieved at the tragedy of his life, reconciles himself to it, at least outwardly, and represses his grief. But in the drama the pang of separation is intolerably acute, and Rāma actually bursts into tears more than once. This intensely human side of Rāma contributes to the heightening of pathos. A hero of epic severity would not appeal to us in the same manner.

One of the first glimpses we get of Sītā reveals her inner nature. When she is asked by Rāma what pastime would please her most, she proposes to go to the forest, although the forest has been so fruitful of misery to her. This shows that she is not a lady to take delight in ordinary conventional pleasures. She is modest, kind, considerate and is in every way a fit helpmate of Rāma. But the most noticeable features of Sītā are her intense love for Rāma and her charity of judgment. She never thinks harshly of Rāma, although she has been wronged by him; rather her love for him seems to grow in separation. Love that can stand the test under such trying circumstances is rare indeed.

There is a remarkable union of innocence and pride of race in Lava. In Sumantra's words, he is characterized both by *darpa* and *saujanya*. A spirit of ardent adventure is seen in him. He fights with Candraketu, not for self-glorification, but only for vindicating the honour of the *Kṣatriya* race, which has been called in question by the heralds of Rāma. He is perfectly fair-minded and kind towards the foe. He bears a wise head on young shoulders. He combines in him the splendour of Rāma and the grace of Sītā, and the royal dignity of both.

One of the main traits of Lakṣmaṇa is his faith in Rāma. He is very tender-hearted, and the extent of his misery for having assisted in the exile of Sītā is indicated by the sigh of relief which escapes him when Sītā is restored to Rāma at last. But, speaking as a whole, Lakṣmaṇa's is not a fully drawn character. This lack of development may be designed, for it brings out Lakṣmaṇa's chief characteristic of self-suppression. He is almost the equal of Rāma in every respect, but he is content to remain in the background.

There is one other personage whose character must be briefly referred to here. He does not appear on the stage at all[1]; but yet his benign influence is felt throughout the play. This is Vālmīki. He is a sage who has renounced the world; but he has not become a recluse. Renunciation has not narrowed his sympathies, but widened them; so much so that he does not

[1] [Except at the very end of the play when he comes forward to present Lava and Kuśa to their parents.—Ed.]

hesitate to undertake what is described as *dhātrīkarma* towards the tender children of Sītā. He is a picture of compassion—a perfected saint using his spiritual power for the good of all, a feature which harmonises so well with his character as a poet.

RASA

The prevailing *rasa* is *karuṇa*, or pathos, which has for its background love—not youthful love, which is apt to be tinged with sensuality, but mature love between two souls that have passed through chastening sorrow and suffering. The subject selected and the dramatic situations invented by the poet are well calculated to impress on the minds of the spectators the depth of the passion depicted. Sītā is a princess naturally tender and deserving of the utmost care. She is utterly innocent and, when exiled, is in a condition of life when pity is excited even in the case of lower beings. To all intents and purposes the separation is absolute and final (*niravadhiḥ*), and the fact that Rāma deliberately exiles her adds to the poignancy of the situation. In the *Meghasandeśa* of Kālidāsa, for example, the separation is to last only for one year, and it is not self-imposed. Yet the grief is intolerable. How much more so should it be in the case of Rāma! The scene is laid mostly in the Daṇḍaka forest which, with its countless associations of Sītā, gives, through Vāsantī, articulate expression, as it were, to Sītā's love for Rāma, and to the sufferings which were her lot to endure for his sake. These circumstances have their natural effect on Rāma. He weeps and faints more than once, and almost goes mad.

We must now indicate how the passion progresses from act to act, as the story moves from one stage to another. The opening scene shows the poet's skill in working on the heart and imagination of the audience. We meet Rāma and Sītā in the rather sudden stillness that follows the coronation. Fate has already prepared the ground for mischief. Sītā is with child, and the old wives of Daśaratha are constrained to leave her. Even Janaka has to go, and Sītā, who has not known the loving caresses of a mother, feels extremely sad at his departure. It is true that there is Rāma with her, and one would think, as indeed Kausalyā did, that his presence was sufficient to comfort her. But fate's irony wills it otherwise. After this effective opening comes the visit of Sītā and Rāma to the picture gallery, which impresses on

CLASSICAL SANSKRIT LITERATURE

We welcome this addition to the *Heritage* series[1] for it so well supplies the long-felt want of a satisfactory text-book on the history of Sanskrit literature which students in our colleges may use. Prof. Macdonell's work on the subject once met this want well enough, but it has remained unrevised for a quarter of a century during which period much new material has accumulated and the need for modifying many an old opinion has arisen. Dr. Winternitz's *Geschichte* is no doubt quite up-to-date; but it is in German and may therefore be left out of account so far as the generality of Indian students are concerned until its promised translation into English, under the auspices of the Calcutta University, is issued. The present work is not so extensive in its scope as either of these. As its title shows, it is confined to the classical period, and even there it leaves out the Drama and stops its review at A.D. 1200. The former deficiency is made good by the author's treatise on the Sanskrit Drama recently announced as published; and nobody need complain of the latter, for whatever is of real worth in Sanskrit literature is more likely to be found before A.D. 1200 than after. Within these limits, it must be said that the work has been admirably done. Owing to the sad lack of definiteness in the matter of dates, the author cannot follow the chronological order in dealing with the subject. So he adopts a classification based upon form and subject-matter, restricting the chronological treatment to each separate head. The first chapter discusses the important question whether Sanskrit or Prakrit was the vehicle of early secular literature in India. Dr. Keith ably maintains that it was Sanskrit and shows that already in the time of Patañjali (150 B.C.) all the main branches of Sanskrit literature were known. The three chapters that follow treat of *Kāvya* or 'Court Poetry' as it is sometimes styled to indicate the circumstances in which it throve and possibly also took its birth. One of these chapters—the best in the book—is entirely devoted to an appreciative consideration of Kālidāsa, the prince of Indian poets. Of the five subsequent chapters, each one takes up for discussion some one or other of the remaining departments of

[1] *Classical Sanskrit Literature.* A. Berriedale Keith, D.C.L., D. Litt., *Association Press, Calcutta.* (*The Heritage of India Series.*)

Sanskrit learning; and the book concludes with an account of the Indian theories of poetry. The information in this last section is somewhat meagre; but we should still feel grateful to the author for recognising the value of this branch and giving it a place in his book. Works on Poetics are not the least important in Sanskrit and as they become better known, we are sure, their worth will be fully appreciated.

One of the questions which Dr. Keith has frequently to consider is that of foreign influence. It is now beyond doubt that such influence is found in one or two spheres of Indian thought, notably Astronomy and Astrology. But the theory of borrowing has been unjustifiably extended to other spheres also. The fact is that in ancient India the best work not only superseded the rest but also led eventually to their disappearance. The superseded works were put aside once for all; and when they were neither copied nor committed to memory, they were generally lost. The result is that the oldest works extant are the best of their kind and it was to account for this peculiar feature that foreign influence was assumed by the early orientalists. But closer study of history has revealed the existence of earlier phases of development; and in a few cases by good luck the very works representing those phases have been recovered. Dr. Keith is fully alive to this aspect of the matter and discusses the theory of borrowing in more than one case as a myth. The value of this theory is well illustrated in the case of Sanskrit Prose Romance in regard to which a certain scholar, who once believed that Greek literature had affected it, came on further consideration to the conculsion that precisely the reverse had taken place. It is not historical questions alone that our author discusses. For the first time in such books, so far as we know, has the attempt been made here to put matters of literary importance first and herein lies the chief value of the book. In the case of every important work mentioned, a summary of the contents is given, often based, as it appears, on a first-hand acquaintance with it; and there is added a judicious estimate of its literary worth. The book, in brief, is both scholarly and sympathetic . . .[1]

[1] *The Mysore University Magazine*, September 1924.

. . . The author shows no eagerness to find foreign influence everywhere. The time indeed is now past when the European orientalist was guided in his investigations by the belief that there was nothing great under the sun which was not Greek in its origin. But the tendency to discover outside influence where there is none in tracing the course of Indian thought has not altogether disappeared; and it is accordingly a relief to find our author willing to allow that two distant communities may develop their thought on parallel lines without necessarily implying any borrowing on either side. The spirit with which he approaches the subject of his study is in general well illustrated by his defence (p. 75) of Sanskrit literature against the charge of 'indelicacy' brought against it by critics with insufficient imagination. We have nothing but praise for this book. . . . The references given as footnotes are not numerous enough. Doubtless this is due to the fact that the book is not intended for the specialist. Yet we cannot help thinking that the insertion of more references would have greatly added to the usefulness of the volume . . .[1]

[1] *Journal of the Karṇāṭaka Sāhitya Parishat*, July 1924.

A HISTORY OF SANSKRIT LITERATURE

The Indian student generally finds it difficult to keep abreast of the progress made in the study of Sanskrit in the West as he knows little of French and German, the two languages in which that progress is mostly recorded. For this reason, he is sure to welcome the appearance of a book in English like the one under review[1] which is quite up-to-date and places the whole harvest, as it were, before him. Its up-to-date and comprehensive character will be well indicated when we mention that even the few additions made to our knowledge of the subject during the time the book was in the press have been noticed at length in the preface. But the work is not a mere compilation of the results of others' investigation. It does indeed summarise them, but it also critically reviews them and has independent opinions to offer on many a topic discussed. Like the other books of the author, the present one also abounds in useful facts; and as for the views expressed in it, we had already a foretaste of them in his shorter work—*Classical Sanskrit Literature*—published a few years ago in the *Heritage of India* series, but naturally they appear here considerably amplified.

The book is divided into three Parts of which the first treats of the language in which is written the literature whose account is to follow in the two remaining Parts. The need for this preliminary essay arises from the fact that there is a difference of opinion among scholars in regard to the vehicle of early secular literature in India as distinguished from the Vedic. Some have held that it was at first entirely in Prakrit. On this theory, works like the *Râmâyaṇa* and the *Mahābhārata* which go back to that early period were originally in Prakrit and were afterwards turned into Sanskrit as that language gained in influence and came to replace Prakrit as the means of literary expression. The theory is finally refuted here, the evidence adduced in that behalf being of overwhelming weight. The several Prakrits, as vernaculars, have no doubt been used all along for popular literature; but it is equally certain that Sanskrit also has throughout served as the medium for expressing

[1] *A History of Sanskrit Literature.* A. Berriedale Keith, D.C.L., D.Litt. *Clarendon Press, Oxford*, 1928.

the higher mind of the community. There is also some doubt about the precise character of the Sanskrit that is used by the classical writers. While it conforms for the most part to the requirements of Pāṇinian grammar, it not infrequently startles us by deviations from it which cannot be satisfactorily explained without assuming, as is done here, a distinction between the language of the priests—'Sanskrit' strictly so termed—and the language that was current in courts and other aristocratic circles. These forms of Sanskrit differ less from each other than either does from Prakrit, but they are sufficiently divergent to be reckoned as two. It is in the latter, which for the sake of convenience is sometimes described as 'epic Sanskrit', that the *Rāmāyaṇa* and the *Mahābhārata* are written. The classical writers are influenced by both these forms of linguistic tradition. Their literary lineage, as is clear from the contents as well as the general artistic make-up of their works, goes back to old epic poets like Vālmīki and it would indeed have been strange if they had not similarly come under their influence on the side of language. Their adherence at the same time to the norm of Pāṇini is to be explained by their great learning which was indispensable for them since their works came to be addressed more and more to expert audiences. The resulting speech Dr. Keith describes as 'singularly beautiful'—purer and more refined than the Sanskrit of the epics but simpler and more elastic than the Pāṇinian form of it. It was first confined to Brahminical writings but gradually extended its scope to Jaina and Buddhistic literature, fields which were at first hostile to it, and continued to be the literary language of all India until Mahomedan rule brought a new language into prominence.

The second part which treats of *belles-lettres* is necessarily the biggest and the most important. Western scholars in their study of this subject have a tendency to stress its historical aspects at the expense of the literary. Questions about authorship, date, authenticity of text, etc., engross their attention but they forget that Sanskrit literature may be valuable for its own sake. It may be that Sanskrit literature, like other literatures, has its own peculiarities which prevent foreign scholars from feeling quite at home with it. But yet with a certain degree of interest in the subject, it will not at all be difficult for them to appreciate it. Prof. Macdonell, while admitting that many beauties in classical Sanskrit poetry are lost to the generality of Western Sanskritists, refers to a 'distinguished scholar' known to him who 'has entered so fully into the spirit of that poetry that he is unable to derive pleasure from any other'. Indian sculpture and painting also were once similarly ignored or even belittled but now, thanks to the efforts of some Indian as well as European scholars, their worth has come to be properly appraised. What has been done in their case remains yet to do for the sister art of poetry. The present work, while not neglecting the historical or the antiquarian side of the study, pays full attention to the literary and artistic qualities of the works discussed. The author brings to this task a sympathetic mind which can appreciate not only the sentiments contained in them but also their more formal and technical excellences such as the blending of sound and sense in style, the elegance of metre and the significance of poetical conventions. This is not to imply that he is blind to the deficiencies of Sanskrit literature; on the contrary he often directs attention to them as for example to the highly tiresome manner of the descriptions in the Prose Romances.

The earlier chapters of this Part are concerned with works of Poetry. The first author to be taken up is Aśvaghoṣa, the renowned Buddhist thinker, who also wrote poetry which in point of artistic value stands next only to that of Kālidāsa. It may seem strange that a history of Sanskrit literature should begin with an account of a Buddhistic poet. That is the result of the neglect and the subsequent loss of the older works in every department of literature owing to their supersession by the best that appeared later. Aśvaghoṣa who preceded Kālidāsa by a couple of centuries himself had, as it is now clear, many predecessors; but their very names have perished and, had it not been for a few quotations from them preserved in ancient works like the *Mahābhāṣya* of Patañjali, we would not have known of them at all. It is true that much difficulty was experienced then in copying and preserving books; but whatever the reason, it proved the bane of Sanskrit literature and we have lost many an old work of value in this way. Even Aśvaghoṣa's poems had fallen into oblivion and their resuscitation is due to the impetus given to Sanskrit study in modern times. The next poet to be considered is Kālidāsa, who, according to the view taken here, wrote about A.D. 400 at Ujjain to which place the Gupta power had shifted by that time from Pāṭaliputra. Then follow brief estimates of lesser epic poets like Bhāravi and Māgha. After Epic poetry we come to the Lyric in which so many Indian poets achieved excellence. The miniature word-pictures in which it abounds have evoked universal admiration and even the Indian dramas owe part of their beauty to their lyrical elegance. Broadly speaking, its theme is either *śṛṅgāra* or *śānti*, the one typified in Kālidāsa, the poet of love and the other, in Bhartṛhari, the prophet of asceticism. The method followed in these chapters is to discuss the dates of the writers, summarize the contents of their chief works, offer remarks on their style and language and then wind up with illustrative quotations from them. Realising, however, the essentially untranslatable character of Sanskrit poetry, our author first gives the selections in the original and then translates them, often adding brief critical remarks. The portions of the book containing the quotations are not the least interesting for, taken together, they serve as an admirable 'Chrestomathie'. The addition of an Index of initial words when the book is next printed will greatly facilitate reference to the large number of beautiful *ślokas* which have thus been brought together here. The chapters that follow treat of works written in prose or in prose intermixed with verse such as the Fables. The method followed here is the same as before and the literary estimates given are of equal value and interest. Another important subject included in this Part is Poetics which, so far as histories of Sanskrit literature go, gets a systematic treatment, for the first time here. Dr. Keith devotes two chapters to it, in the first of which he deals generally with the aims and achievements of the Sanskrit poet and in the second, specifically with the various theories of poetry that were formulated from time to time by Indian literary critics. The theories are of great interest—especially that known as the theory of *Dhvani*, which holds that suggestion marks the true process of poetry. It means that the ultimate content of poetry baffles direct expression, and accordingly values suggestion not as a mere trick of style but as the *sole* means of communicating what is otherwise incommunicable. The theory is characteristically Indian and may remind one of the Vedāntic view of Brahman which words and thoughts, as it is said, alike fail to grasp.

The last part is devoted to scientific or technical literature such as Astronomy, Law and Grammar. It stands on a footing different from the one so far considered for its appeal is not aesthetic and it cannot therefore be subjected to an artistic judgment. Nor is it possible in a single section of a book to devote to its various branches—representing as they do the result of so much specialization—the attention that is due to their importance. Some of them like Philosophy, for example, require independent treatises if they are to be adequately considered. Yet it is a great advantage to have in the same book an account, however slight it may be in some cases, of the whole of the literature written in the classical language. Such an account we have in the present work and together with the author's volume on the Drama already issued by the same publishers, it gives a splendid survey of the entire range of classical Sanskrit literature. . .[1]

[1] *The Mysore University Magazine*, March 1929.

THE STUDY OF SANSKRIT

* * * *

It seems to me particularly fitting that this Association should be formed at the present moment, for there has just come to life the University of Mysore—a University which in its scheme of studies gives to Sanskrit an emphasis which it has not hitherto received in Southern India. Sanskrit is now recognized not only as a Second language alternative to Kannada, Telugu and Tamil but also as an Optional subject alongside of Science, History and Philosophy. This double place in the curriculum which the University has not vouchsafed to any other subject raises the expectation that the cause of Sanskrit education here is at last coming to its own and the formation of a Sanskrit Association by the students at such a time may be taken to indicate an earnest desire on their part to fully utilize the opportunities that will be offered to them.

Why is it, we may ask ourselves, that we value so highly associations like the present one? The answer to this question must rest chiefly on the fact that the business of such associations lies outside the routine work of the class. Excluding for the moment the absolutely indolent, people may, I think, be divided into two classes—those that are satisfied with doing the minimum work required of them, and those that do not rest until they have exerted themselves to the utmost of their ability. It is the latter that realize the serious aspects of life and it is through their efforts that human society is enabled to move forward. When students take part in founding such associations or in furthering their interests, they give proof of their desire to belong to the second of the above classes rather than to the first. They show that they possess a spirit of self-reliance and a capacity for concerted action; they show that they can resist that 'craving for repose' which is the blight of so much of early promise.

Yet it is not for such high significance only that these associations should be valued. They have immediate uses also to serve, for they extend and supplement the work of the class in a manner in which no other organization can do. Class-teaching has many advantages over individual teaching, especially when the number of students seeking instruction is large. But this system has the defects of its qualities. A course of study drawn up for many must be uniform and a method of teaching intended for several must be adjusted to the capacity of the less efficient among them. Despite any efforts that may be made for paying individual attention, all simultaneous instruction is bound to suffer from these defects. But in an association like the present one, the conditions of study are far different. Here every student selects that subject which appeals to him most and although receiving guidance from the teacher, carries on his study primarily by himself. This calls forth his individuality and stimulates independent effort. The student acquires from the beginning habits of self-culture which will make it easier for him to follow some intellectual pursuit in later life. At present, in far too many cases, study ceases with graduation.

Having so far dwelt upon the usefulness of such associations in general, I may now offer a few observations on the scope and method of the work that may be done by your Association. The first point that I would like to mention under this head is, that, although each student may select for investigation that subject which lies nearest his heart, the work of the Association, as a whole, should be comprehensive. Do not allow yourselves to be always dealing with one class of subjects only, however important they may be. Broadly speaking, the subjects that should engage your attention will fall into two divisions—linguistic and literary. Each of these divisions has its own importance and I would ask you to pay equal attention to both, overcoming the tendency, noticeable in the Sanskrit student, to leave alone the linguistic aspect of his study. As regards literary subjects I should particularly mention one point. We owe a great deal to the European Sanskritist. It was he that opened our eyes to the possibilities of useful study outside the beaten tracks of traditional scholarship. But, speaking generally, Western scholars have hitherto neglected to deal with the artistic side of Sanskrit literature or have assumed its value to be too slight to be worth their trouble. That the aesthetic value of Sanskrit literature is considerable may be shown on the evidence of the few Europeans themselves who have devoted their attention to it. Prof. Macdonell refers in his book on *Sanskrit Literature* to a distinguished scholar of his acquaintance who (to use the words of the book) 'has entered so fully into the spirit of Sanskrit poetry that he is unable to derive pleasure from any other'. There is reason for the neglect of this phase of Sanskrit study by Europeans who are unfamiliar with Indian conditions and who cannot understand the full significance of Indian mythology in which so much of Sanskrit poetry is steeped. But there can be no excuse in your case for, being Indians, you can fully appreciate Indian sentiments and ideals. No one claims perfection for Sanskrit poetry; but it has distinctive features of its own and its best specimens are well-adapted to be a source of inspiration and of joy. It behoves Indian students to devote adequate attention to this subject even from their early days so that some of them may later do for Sanskrit poetry what is already being done by scholars for ancient Indian painting and sculpture. In estimating the artistic worth of Sanskrit literature you will derive much help from the numerous works in Sanskrit on poetics. They sometimes give you an insight into the nature and aim of poetry which it is difficult to find elsewhere in works on literary criticism.

While linguistic and literary subjects occupy your first attention, there are other subjects also in which you should feel specially interested. Under the scheme of study adopted by the Mysore University you specialize in two subjects in the Degree course—an arrangement which brings Sanskrit into close association with History and Philosophy. Accordingly the subjects that deserve your attention next should be Indian History and Indian Philosophy—each of which offers a vast field for useful work. But whatever be the subject, linguistic, literary, historical or philosophical, do not rest content with merely collecting the results obtained by others. You will necessarily familiarise yourselves with those results; but even before doing so, you should as learners begin an independent investigation—so far, I mean, as is compatible with your attainments. Thus if 'Kalidasa's Art' be your subject, you must first set about examining for yourselves his dramas and poems and when you have formulated your views at least roughly, you may consult whatever you may find written by others on the subject. It is only thus that you will be able to understand the exact bearing of the observations made by others; and it is only thus that you will be able to arrive at well-reasoned convictions regarding the subject of your study. I am not recommending this course for the value of the results you may attain by it. Even in maturer years it is given only to a few to obtain results of value and make additions to knowledge. From your standpoint it is the spirit of independent research that matters; not its results. And every student must cultivate that spirit while at college. Lessing, the German poet and critic, is reported to have said that 'if the Almighty were to offer him the truth in one hand and the search after the truth in the other, he would choose the hand that held the search after truth.'

The next point I would urge upon your attention is the necessity for thoroughness in your study, especially because that quality has always distinguished Sanskrit learning. Specialization has ever been the dominant feature of the Pandit; and for grasp, for accuracy and consistency of thought, he is unsurpassed. His knowledge is so systematically arranged and his exposition of it is so finished that he appears to have made a fine art of study. He has so far handed down the ancient learning with scrupulous care. But he is now rapidly disappearing and if we, of the present generation do not follow his example in thoroughness of study and if we do not maintain his standard of knowledge we shall be losing for posterity one of the precious characteristics of our learning and will thereby be doing a disservice to the country. Already the belief is gaining ground—not altogether without reason I fear—that the English-knowing student of Sanskrit is shallow and superficial. It is your prime duty, particularly of such as are specializing in Sanskrit, to remove this stigma by the earnestness and diligence with which you apply yourselves to your study.

While retaining all that is excellent in the old-type learning, you should aim at more than a mere reproduction of it. First, you must learn to look at every question you study from the standpoint of its whole history. This is an aspect of enquiry which the Pandit may be said to have ignored altogether. His scholarship is undoubtedly thorough and exact but only so far as it goes; and on the historical side it does not go very far.

The consequence is that when you ask the Pandit to trace the development of an idea or the changes in the form of an expression, he fails altogether. He is generally satisfied with an explanation of a thing as it is found in a particular stage of its evolution. He does not ordinarily recognize anything as having passed through successive stages of growth or decay. In other words, time finds no place in his conception of knowledge. It is the duty of the modern student to supplement this deficiency in the old learning and I may illustrate how this may be done by means of one or two simple examples.

We have in Sanskrit a word *vigra* of which the meaning is thus defined by Amara: *vigro vigatanāsikaḥ*. We get no explanation of this word in Pāṇini, but one of his followers, probably Kātyāyana, by whose time the word must have come into ordinary use, explains its formation by stating that *gra*, the second syllable in it, is a substitute for *nāsikā*. It is hard for us, with our notion of etymology, to understand how the single syllable *gra* came to take the place of the trisyllabic *nāsikā* with which it has no phonetic kinship whatever. Can we suggest any satisfactory derivation? We can, if we only recognize what is a commonplace of modern Philology, that languages change constantly and, as a result of change, show growth or decay in their various elements. The recognition of this truth will help us to connect the syllable *gra* in the word we are considering with the well-known root *ghrā* which means 'to smell' and which is found in the word *vyāghra*, 'tiger', literally 'the smelling animal'. The original form of our word was probably *vighra* of which the second syllable underwent, in course of time, a modification in pronunciation and became de-aspirated. It is thus not a substitute for *nāsikā* as Kātyāyana has it, but only a worn out form of *ghrā*. Although the explanation is so easy, the ancient grammarian missed it, because he ignored the possibility of change in language and thought that linguistic facts continued, through all time, to retain, what he assumed to be, their ready-made forms.

I have illustrated my point by taking the *form* of a word into consideration. It is equally easy to give an example where the change affects its *meaning* or *content*. All of us know the old story about Indra clipping the wings of mountains which, as it is said, could fly in olden days and played havoc by alighting now in one place and now in another. The very absurdity of this story suggests that it must have had a different significance once. The history of a single word clears up the mystery. The Sanskrit word *parvata* consists of two elements—*parva*, 'a knot' or 'section' and *ta*, a suffix signifying possession. The word thus means anything that is in sections and is an appropriate designation for a line of clouds or a range of hills. As a matter of fact we find the word used in both these senses in the *Ṛgveda*. The term was probably originally applied to a class of objects that answered a certain description; but in course of time became narrowed down to its present meaning of 'mountain'; as, for example, has been the case with the English word 'deer' which once meant 'wild animal' but is now applied to one particular class of animals. From this explanation, it is obvious that what the story once said of Indra and clouds has gradually come to be erroneously associated with Indra and mountains. Indra is the Vedic god of rain who cleaves the clouds and releases the water. What wonder if the fancy of the Vedic Indians represented the scudding clouds as flying from Indra and their ultimate stoppage as due to the clipping of their wings. Thus by comparing the meanings of *parvata* in two different periods in the history of the language we discover that the current form of the story is due to a discrepancy of interpretation.

These two illustrations will, I trust, make clear what I mean by saying that you should look at everything you study in the light of its history. The traditional explanation in both these cases is unconvincing and therefore arouses our curiosity and leads us to investigation. But often, even when our enquiry is not historical, we get plausible explanations but we must be careful not to take them for correct explanations, for we shall not know where they are deficient until we resort to historical analysis. We should never feel satisfied with the explanation of single stages but push it back as far as we can, for we cannot know the part aright until we have known the whole.

In a second direction also the deficiency of the old scholarship has to be made good by modern study. By the very nature of the conditions under which the old Pandit lived, he was unable to bring to bear upon his study a wide knowledge reaching beyond things Indian. The modern student, on the other hand, has vast opportunities for extending his knowledge and it is therefore his duty to make the study of Sanskrit comparative. The science of language has established a close kinship among communities inhabiting various parts of the globe and unless we compare ancient Indian thoughts and modes of expression with those of kindred communities of the past, we cannot be said to have arrived at the truth. I may illustrate the advantages of pursuing the comparative method of study by means of a well-known example. The Sanskrit words *sura* and *asura* are quite familiar to us. *Asura* is commonly explained as the opposite of *sura*—*a* + *sura*, i.e., 'not god', i.e., 'demon'. So long as we restrict our enquiry to Sanskrit literature of the classical period, i.e., to works produced during the past twenty-five centuries nearly, no suspicion arises as regards the current explanation of these two words. But when we extend our search farther back and examine the *Ṛgveda*, we find the term *asura* used, contrary to our expectation, to glorify gods such as Varuṇa who is one of the most benevolent of Vedic gods. What could be the explanation of this unexpected use? The old Pandit who interpreted the Veda, also realized the difficulty but he could not get beyond the traditional explanation of *asura* and therefore assumed that the word applied to the gods in the Veda—although bearing the same form—was distinct from the common word meaning 'demon'. According to him the two were homonyms, i.e., words with the same form but with different meanings. The Vedic word was referred to the root *as* 'to throw'. Sāyaṇa thus paraphrases it in one place—*asuraḥ aniṣṭakṣepaṇaśīlaḥ*, i.e., 'able to throw away or remove misery or what is disagreeable.' We cannot help feeling that this interpretation is far-fetched and artificial. The modern scholar, on the other hand, with his more extensive knowledge of Indo-Germanic literature gets light upon this dark point from a quarter least suspected by the Pandit, for the Zend or old Persian Scriptures contain the word *ahura* used similarly in addressing gods. By applying a simple law of phonetic correspondence between Zend and Vedic—commonly illustrated by the pair of words *Sindhu* and *Hindu*—we see that this word *asura* is only a variant of *ahura*. The inference is that the bad sense which attaches to *asura* did not originally belong to it at all but was imported into it subsequently, though we cannot now say why. When once the word *asura* became established in its new sense, its initial syllable *a* was easily mistaken for the negative prefix and a spurious word *sura* came into use with the meaning of 'god' the opposite of 'demon'. Thus we see that a comparision of *asura* with a word found in a cognate language has disclosed to us that the current explanation is as far from the truth as it can possibly be. It was not *asura* that was derived from *sura* but it was the reverse that happened. Instances of this kind may be multiplied but this example is sufficient to indicate the necessity, in the interests of truth, for pursuing the comparative method in studying Sanskrit.

The application of this method to the study of Sanskrit presents certain difficulties to the Indian student for it presupposes an acquaintance with other Indo-Germanic languages and literatures and there is no provision now in Colleges for teaching even the more important European classical and modern languages. We may hope that these difficulties will be removed in course of time. Till they are removed the student must fight his way through them as best as he can. Although it is difficult now to learn European languages, there are other kindred languages which can be learnt with relatively less trouble. There is Persian for example and there are the northern Sanskritic vernaculars like Bengali and Hindi, a knowledge of which will be of great use in dealing with Sanskrit Philology. The equipment of the Sanskrit student in respect of linguistic knowledge has hitherto been very meagre and the useful work he may do has accordingly become considerably limited.

In the scheme of studies now sanctioned by the Mysore University French is included among second languages and provision for teaching it will soon be made. I trust that many of you will take advantage of this opportunity to widen your outlook on Sanskrit study.

My reference to the historical and comparative methods will indeed be incomplete if I do not lay special stress on the spirit with which they should be pursued. Whichever be the method we apply to a particular case, we must exercise the maximum amount of care in the collection as well as in the appreciation of the evidence on which we are to base our conclusions; otherwise they will be worth no more than the conjectures of the man in the street. We should never yield to the temptation of accepting our data without proper verification and we should never draw conclusions without a due consideration of the evidence for them. In one word our investigation must be critical. It is this critical attitude that gives our investigation a truly scientific aspect. The old question of the relative merits of science and the 'humanities', as instruments of education, is periodically raised but it is overlooked that it is possible to give a scientific bent to literary studies by following right methods. After all the primary object of a liberal education is not the acquisition of either scientific or literary facts but the proper disciplining of the mind and of the soul. If the sort of discipline that science affords can be secured by means of literature as well much of the bitterness that ranges on either side of the controversy becomes meaningless.

I have so far alluded only to one side of your work, which may be called the cultural side because it helps the proper training of the mind and the acquisition of the right type of knowledge. There is also another kind of work which, under existing circumstances, your Association is expected to do. I refer to your activities in the direction of popularising Sanskrit study among the students. I am glad you have not confined membership of this Association to Sanskrit students but have thrown it open to all. You may include in your programme lectures on Sanskrit language and literature and on Indian antiquities generally intended for the non-Sanskrit student. In course of time some of you may perhaps devote part of your leisure to the teaching of Sanskrit to those that feel interested in it—a kind of altruistic activity in which another Society in this college has already set such a good example. Any how, every member of this Association must feel it his duty to do something in the way of increasing the interest of students in Sanskrit. Until a few years ago, the Madras University recognized Sanskrit as an alternative Second language and owing to this 'partial compulsion' a due proportion of students used to learn Sanskrit. With the introduction of the revised regulations by that University Sanskrit was transferred to the head of Optional subjects and students immediately withdrew from Sanskrit study. It is a pity that the moment compulsion is removed students should desert their classical language. The chief reason for this apathy is that Sanskrit lacks that conventional value which current ideals of education have set upon other subjects and conventional value alone, unfortunately, determines at present the attitude of our students towards subjects of study. Reverence for the past which is a necessary element in patriotism springs from a proper understanding of the past and for a proper understanding of India's past, a knowledge of Sanskrit is essential. This aspect of the matter at least, if none other, should appeal to our young men and I trust that through the exertions of your Association a larger number of them will be attracted to the study of Sanskrit.

• • • •